A Walk on the 'Weird' Side in Nebraska

Harriett McFeely

A Walk on the 'Weird' Side in Nebraska
by Harriett McFeely

Copyright © 2021, Harriett Rose McFeely.

All Rights Reserved.

No part of the material protected by this notice may be reproduced or utilized in any form, electronic, photographic, mechanical, or otherwise, except for brief excepts quoted in connection with reviews, without written permission from the copyright holder.

Bigfoot Crossroads of America

Museum and Research Center

1205 E. 42nd St. Hastings, NE 68901

Printed in the United States of America

ISBN: 978-0-9838604-2-6

Copyright for certain images contained in this work is owned and retained by their respective creators or publishers. These include works by Donald Monroe, Igor Burtsev and M.K. Davis, and others as well as newspaper articles used by permission. Certain maps, weather data, and photographic images produced by the United States Government are in the public domain. Certain historical images are in the public domain, and others are in the public domain by declaration of their respective creators. Copyright for these as individual images is not claimed here.

Images of newspaper articles are used herein as components of the author's research to establish that certain views were expressed at certain times, and do not necessarily encompass all views of the respective publications.

Printing version 1.03 incorporating minor corrections

Transcription, design and initial layout Tamara Steir

Final layout and production Thad Mauney

MANY THANKS TO RUTHLEDGE AND SOLDON

FOR BEING A HUGE INSPIRATION TO ME AS

I WROTE THIS BOOK! WITHOUT YOU,

I WOULD NEVER HAVE BEEN ABLE

TO WRITE THE FIRST WORD...

Much Love,
Harriett,
The Bigfoot Lady

Contents

A Walk on the 'Weird' Side in Nebraska

Foreword	ix
Preface	xi
Thank You!	xii
To Begin	1
Memorial Day Weekend	3
Garrison Hits the Front Page	5
The Investigation Begins	7
Whose Hair??	9
Witnesses of the 'Weird'	10
Museum Investigation Team	14
The Horses and the Flag	21
The Experts	23
Mr. Don Monroe	25
Dr. Igor Burtsev	26
The Braided Horses - Australia	33
The Braided Horses - USA	35
The Braided Horses - Missouri	37
The Braided Horses - Nebraska	42
Mr. Richard Soule	44
Mr. Scott Barta	49
Mr. Ron Morehead	51
Mr. Joe Taylor	53
Mr. M. K. Davis	54
More Evidence	58

Contents

A Walk on the 'Weird' Side in Nebraska

Breaking News! (In the last 100 Years!) 60
Bob Sautter 64
The Killing Fields 67
Flag Retirement Ceremony 71
13 Flags 73
Don Monroe - U.S. Navy 78
Bruce - U.S. Navy 84
Joe - U.S. Air Force 85
Little Sioux Baskets 87
Garrison, NE, Flag - 2020 90
Washington, DC, Flag - 1917 91
Weather Reports - 1917 96
Weather Reports - 2020 99
Grand Island, Nebraska 106
Braided Windsocks, Marcola, Oregon 108
Braided Windsocks 114
Opposable Thumbs? 115
Braided Ropes 116
A Historic Flag Mystery 118
Nebraska Giants 121
Ron Morehead 124
Thoughts 125
Conclusions 128
AND 129

Foreword

    Most books contain at least some things the reader can relate to—HOWEVER, not this manuscript! It is a very strange anomaly, something far from normal, peculiar, WEIRD… In my case, this true story has NEVER been documented before. In order to fully understand this story, one first needs to understand the author, Harriett McFeely, and her talented MUSEUM CREW that has done the research on a very unusual bizarre event in Nebraska history. Harriett, the curator of the now famed BIGFOOT MUSEUM in Hastings, Nebraska, brings to light the absolute message that supposed fiction is documented as a true fact. And fact, eternally remains exactly what it is…There is no small lack of imagination here. All of the events are true, exactly as investigated by Harriett and her MUSEUM researchers.

    This is a MUST-READ account occurrence as if it were 'dreamed up' to alarm the public. Nothing like this in my experience has ever been explained before.

    Harriett was born to MUSEUMS and logistics. She is highly methodical; a dedicated investigator reminiscent of Arthur Conan Doyle, Sherlock Holmes and Dr. Watson, all combined. Sherlock leaves no stone alone - all possibilities are unraveled. Harriett said, "Don, this is a very strange story that needs to be written in a book." And, she has done it!

    Enjoy your journey, complete with twists and turns; and lots of mysteries…AND - as you read this remember, this is a true 'WEIRD' story!

Don Monroe

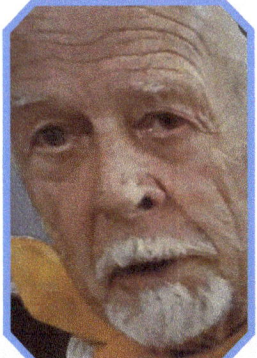

60 + Years Researcher/ Explorer & Author

 # Preface

This book contains actual accounts by real people based on personal interviews, newspaper archives and other documented resources.

With a growing number of researchers and individuals who collect and report '**WEIRD**' happenings we have had to narrow down our field to professionals and our top **NEBRASKA** experts, due to the content of this true story. As such, it is important to state that the accounts we have presented here were carefully selected on their merits of credibility, location to the site, dates and the limited amount of information collected.

We believe that this will be an ongoing story…just as it began…

Harriett,
The Bigfoot Lady

Thank You!

In Jeremiah 29:9

It says, "For I know the plans I have for you, declares the Lord: plans to prepare you and not harm you, plans to give you a hope, and a future."

Thank you, Lord, for this fantastic 'Trip'!! I BELIEVE you have plans for me...but you certainly surprised me with this one!

Thank you, Lord, for the FLAG in Garrison, Nebraska. What a MIRACLE. Thank you Mr. Jim Daro and his family, who trusted me accepted me, helped me and encouraged me.

Thank you, Lord, for the citizens of Garrison, the American Legion members, and the V.F.W. members.

Thank you, Lord, for my constant companion, "Snooksie." Thank you Lord, for waking me up early to given me a name for a new chapter, a sentence, or a whole paragraph! Even a whole chapter!

Thank you, Lord, for reminding me of names and for given me pictures. Thank you for the scientists, researchers, the people with 'Boots on the GROUND', conference attendees and Museum guests who have given me encouragement, knowledge and ideas that I would NEVER have thought of...

Thank you, Lord, for the SPECIAL PEOPLE in my life. I KNOW THAT YOU SENT THEM!! We BRAINSTORM for all of your plans you have for us; CONFERENCES, THE MUSEUM, SPEAKERS, and Special Exhibits!

 # Thank You!

Thank you, Lord for Don Monroe who has called me every day for month, to make sure I am 'OK,' to give me a 'pep talk' and encouragement! He called even on his worst days, even when he was battling the effects of a COPPERHEAD SNAKE bite! It is very exciting to know that in one person's eyes, my book is on the New York Times Bestsellers List! He is a real friend.

Tamara Stier came on board in October. SHE SAVED ME! I know and believe that God sent her to me! Tamara came on a Sunday afternoon with her family to the Museum. We instantly began to talk (like old friends...) BUT, when she saw the GARRISON FLAG, she was IMMEDIATELY 'HOOKED'!! (Thank you Lord). Ideas began popping into her head: projects, research ideas, setting up my picture magnifier on my phone! She took over typing MY ENTIRE BOOK, AND...her husband, Trent, helped with all the beautiful, colored pictures that tell a story all by themselves. Tamara is a professional RESEARCH ANALYST and she brought information to this book that I would NEVER have had, or thought about... In addition, to everything she and Trent have done, she's also becoming a valued friend. Thank you, Tamara!!

Debbie Waters has been my best friend for over 40 years. She has always been there for me, without fail...and this journey is no exception... (even though she is not a BIGFOOT BELIEVER – not yet...) She has helped me daily. She manages the Museum's finances, bring me things I need (that I didn't know I need), does computer and telephone work that is like CHINESE to me... She is a great listener and is very logical and level-headed. I cannot even image my life without her by my side!! Thank you Debbie!! And thank you God for sending Debbie to me!

Thanks to all of you for giving me this once in a lifetime opportunity!

And thank you God!

Much Love,

Harriett, The Bigfoot Lady

A Walk on the 'Weird' Side in Nebraska

This is weird. Who or what caused it?

To Begin...

Margo's 'Weird' Story

This is a chronicle of true events that has been slowly UNRAVELING AND EXPLODING throughout Central Nebraska.

On June 12, 2020 Margo Hlavac visited Hastings, Nebraska to see the BIGFOOT– CROSSROADS OF AMERICA MUSEUM AND RESEARCH CENTER.

Many times I walk through the MUSEUM with guests and tell them information, facts and stories about our many exhibits. AND, one important word I always teach my guests is 'WEIRD'! I want them to pay close attention when they either say or hear this word!

This is the one word that stands out when folks share their BIGFOOT stories with me - 'WEIRD'! Often times I have heard people say,

"I heard something really WEIRD", or "I saw something really WEIRD..." So, this is a word that I really pay close attention to, always. As one friend said to me, "If something is WEIRD, chances are it's WEIRD!"

I have heard some interesting 'WEIRD' stories about Bigfoot, UFOs, ghosts, giants, and other things, and I really listen. So, when Margo came to our MUSEUM with a 'Weird' story to tell about an incident that had recently occurred in her small town of Garrison, Nebraska, population 54, I was all ears...

Margo Hlavac

To Begin...

The following is a true story of a famous, well-used flag that was flown in a small Nebraska town for many years. Its use was limited to just two days each year: Memorial Day and Veterans Day. The remainder of the year it was lovingly folded and stored in the homes of the caretakers of the cemetery.

However, this year the flag was flown an extra day because of a proclamation made by President Donald Trump to honor the many health care professionals and first responders working tirelessly across our country on behalf of our citizens who had contracted the COVID-19 virus. This was in addition to all departed veterans and family members.

It was Jim Daro's 'Uncle George' Daro who had donated the large flag (approximately 5' x 7') to the Garrison Cemetery Association in 1991, over 29 years ago. Uncle George has since passed away, but his entire family has continued the tradition he so proudly started of flying the flag.

Jim's dad - Walter, George, Edwin, John & Norman.
(left to right)

Each year, many members of the Daro Family join in this annual celebration. Several of them tend to the cemetery year round, mowing the grass, trimming the trees and placing flags on the graves of fallen veterans.

Garrison Cemetery

Recent rains had 'greened' the grass, and the flowers were in full bloom.

E.J. Hlavac

E. J. Hlavac raised the flag on the 30 foot pole about 7pm on Friday night, May 22nd of Memorial Day weekend. It was flown at half mast, situated about 15 feet from the ground. This was to designate respect for both the flag and the first responders being honored.

 Memorial Day Weekend

It was Saturday afternoon about 5pm May 23rd. When Margo Hlavac, noticed one of her chickens had died. As was her custom, she put the chicken in a box and took it to Kezan Creek, which runs behind the cemetery, where she "recycles" her fallen fowl. She leaves their bodies near the creek for the raccoons and other animals to feast on. As she strolled by the cemetery, she couldn't help but notice how beautiful everything looked.

By this time, all of the tasks were completed, and the flag was gently blowing in the breeze. She thought to herself: "The flag really looked pretty today." It perfectly complimented the cemetery decor, with grass freshly mowed and trimmed and family members had been placing flowers on each grave. For the moment, everything was peaceful, quiet and beautiful…

FOR A WHILE…

For 29 consecutive years the flag had flown proudly from sunrise to sunset on Memorial Day, less than 24 hours. On this year, however, in May 2020, the flag flew overnight on Memorial Day weekend.

 # Memorial Day Weekend

On Sunday Morning, May 24th, Juli, Jim's daughter, found the flag after mass about 10:45 am. The flag was discovered torn to shreds, destroyed, some 36 hours after it had been raised and 15 hours after many people had seen it intact.

The red and white strips that had been torn in two measured approximately 4¼ wide, and they had been torn in half lengthwise in long strips from the blue background with the white stars to the very end of the flag.

Near the blue field, or 'canton,' two red and white strips were pulled together into one long strip and tied with a small, tight, knot, about the size of a marble. Then, the red and white strips were braided together from the top to the bottom (end) of the flag.

A few inches from the far end, a large knot, roughly the size of a tennis ball, was tied several times, VERY TIGHTLY!! Upon learning of its demise, the Cemetery Association promptly replaced the tattered flag with another for the remainder of the holiday weekend.

Strips are clearly braided.

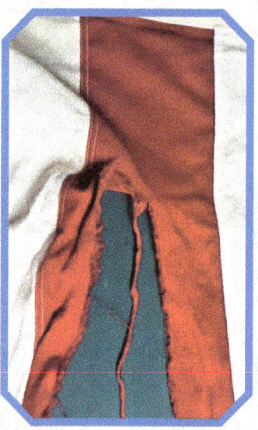

See how bright the colors are??

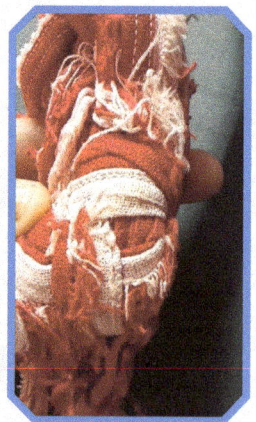

Large knot.

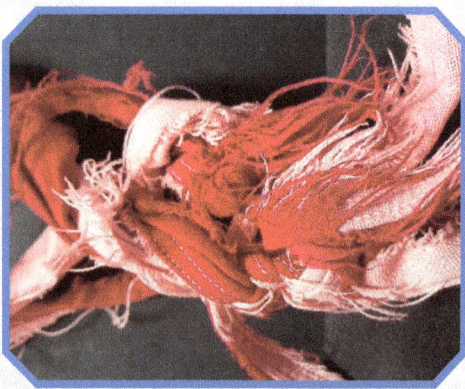

Large knot.

Strips are braided.

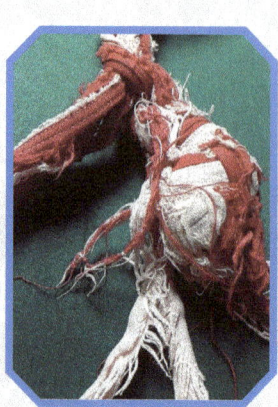

Large knot.

 Garrison Hits the Front Page

Jim Daro

Butler County Sheriff's Department

Jim Daro was mystified…He took the flag's remains to the Butler County Sheriff's office to report the incident. A deputy sheriff viewed the flag and said he would file a report and tell Sheriff Dion.

The sheriff telephoned Jim later with his theory about the flag. He initially concluded that the flag had been damaged by either extreme weather conditions or "misplaced good intentions." The Sheriff had not actually seen the flag at that time.

The Banner-Press

Torn flag may have been victim of storm, misplaced intentions

Hannah Schrodt   Jun 17, 2020   0

1 of 2

During a flag retirement ceremony held Sunday, members of the David City American Legion and VFW showed the crowd a destroyed American Flag found over Memorial Day weekend. Butler County Sheriff Tom Dion said he believed the flag to be the victim of extreme weather and misplaced good intentions.

Hannah Schrodt

Hannah Schrodt, The Banner-Press, David City, Nebraska, June 17, 2020.

Garrison Hits the Front Page

Hannah Schrodt, The Banner-Press, David City, Nebraska, June 15, 2020, used by permission.

Later, on Flag Day, June 14th, during a Flag Retirement Ceremony in David City, Nebraska, members of the local VFW and American Legion chapters showed visitors the torn flag that had been braided, twisted and wrapped at the ends!!

Like the Sheriff, Jim Daro initially believed the flag had fallen victim to the heavy storms that had visited the area that day. BUT, upon further inspection, he noticed the tattered ends were braided!! Now he is confused and undecided…

Tightly twisted and wrapped at the ends...

 The Investigation Begins

VFW Commander, Larry Sabata said he personally would offer a $200.00 reward to anyone who had information concerning the flag's desecration.

The Flag Retirement Ceremony on Sunday, June 14th was shorter than planned, and the ceremony was only partially held. More than 200 flags were scheduled for retirement and burning at the conclusion of the ceremony. Instead, strong winds that pummeled the area made it unsafe to burn the retired flags.

That part of the ceremony was rescheduled for Veterans Day, November 11th.

All members of our Research/Investigation team were so HAPPY because the strong winds saved this most unusual flag from being burned! Because of this, the mysteriously braided flag was spared.

Details about its unusual mutilation are well chronicled in the local newspapers, corroborating Margo Hlavac's 'WEIRD' story that she told me!

VFW Commander Larry Sabata

Team Members

Harriett McFeely
Museum Curator
Researcher
& Investigator

Tamara Stier
Research Analyst
MUFON Field
Investigator

Art Wach
16 Year Tracker,
Researcher &
Investigator

 The Investigation Begins

On Wednesday, July 8th, 2020, Team Members of my Bigfoot Museum Staff, including myself, drove to Garrison to do a complete investigation of the strange braiding incident ourselves.

Little Waters Bar & Grill

Upon inspection, it became obvious to all of us that the flag had been torn intentionally and then braided into long strips with a large knot tied on the end of each individual braid. Some sections of the strips were only about 2 inches long, and measuring only about ¼ the size of a pencil. The flag quite obviously, WAS NOT A VICTIM of any type of "extreme weather conditions..."

These sections were also braided with a very small knot on each end. Several strings were twisted together with red and white strings wrapped and knotted around them.

Harriett & friends inspecting the flag.

Jim Daro

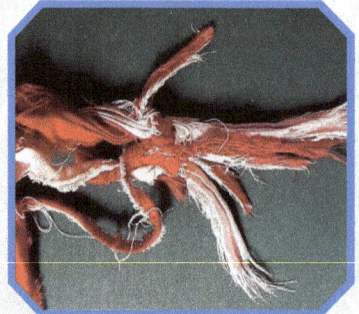
Large knot.

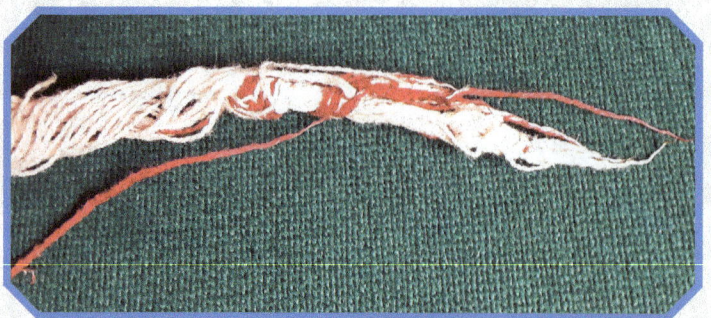
White string twisted up with red wrapped around.

Whose Hair??

Adding to the mystery of the flag, a MUSEUM staff member, discovered six unidentified hairs attached to the flag. They were a light, reddish-brown in color and each measured about 1 inch long. Their texture was soft; with shapes both straight and slightly curly.

I personally checked with both Jim and Margo to see if either one had a dog or cat that was a light reddish-brown color that may have left the hairs. Margo had a cat named Steve, who was all white, a different color from the hairs found on the front and back of the flag. Jim did not have a cat or a dog.

The hairs still remain a mystery to this day…

In the future, we plan to have these hairs DNA tested.

Margo's cat 'Steve'.

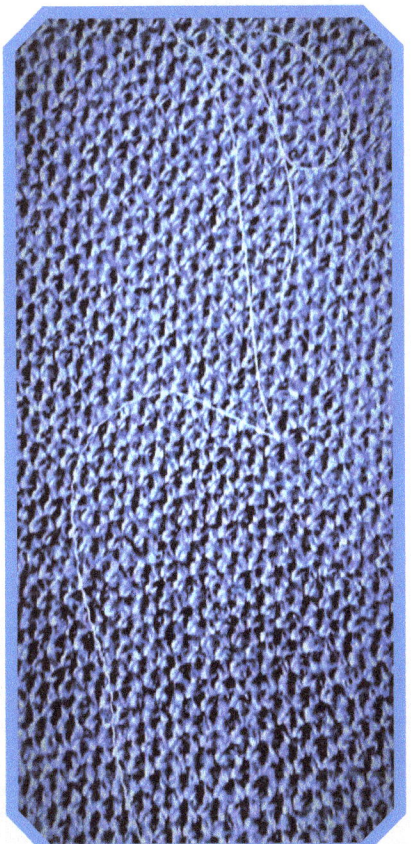

Hairs from the flag.

Unknown hairs from Colorado. Donated by Mr. Mike Johnson and Scott Barta, Founders of S.I.R., Sasquatch Investigation of the Rockies.

 Witnesses of the 'Weird'

While in Garrison, a Museum member and I personally interviewed several residents of the small community who had witnessed 'WEIRD HAPPENINGS' locally over Memorial Day weekend.

Maxine, 'Max' is a lady who lives across the street from the City Park. Walking it's one square block each morning, she routinely tidies up the park by collecting any twigs and branches she comes upon that had fallen the previous night.

'Max' and Jim.

While embarking on her walk, about 8 a.m., on Sunday, May 24th, she came upon a large limb measuring about 4 or 5 inches in diameter, that had been partially broken off the tree near its trunk.

It originated some 15 feet above the ground.

Near the end of that limb there were five or six lower hanging branches (about 5 feet in length) that were still growing from the main big limb. The branches were all grouped together and then braided to the end of the main, primary branch!!

Ends of branches braided together.

Broken limb in Garrison.

The strangest thing about the large, dangling broken limb was that the bark was twisted around and around, though still attached to the main trunk. It didn't look like the typical break where a branch splits as it is bent down. And also, this was the only observable broken limb in the entire park! Other than this, not even a single leaf seemed out of place or blown down from the night before…

Typical Nebraska tree breaks.

 Witnesses of the 'Weird'

The next thing that 'Max' noticed were the metal and wire cages that had been placed around two newly planted small trees. The cages were put there to protect the little trees from 'nicks' caused by the lawn mower. However, on this Sunday morning, the two wire cages were both lifted up and tossed about three or four feet away from the little sapling trees coming to rest near the big tree with the braided branches!

Wire cages.

Jolene, Jim Daro's wife, also reported a "WEIRD HAPPENING…" her daughter, Jenna and two granddaughters; Morgan and Karissa were going to walk home from Jim and Jolene's after a short visit.

Jolene

They walked toward their home; a short stroll only about 1½ blocks away; adjacent to the cemetery. A walk they had taken many times before… as they walked, they heard what they described as a terrible sound, *a scream*, half howl, half growl, all combined! Like a dog – and a rooster… Jenna said, "IT WAS REALLY LOUD… AND, VERY CLOSE!!"

It terrified them, because it was unlike any sound they had EVER heard before. It was certainly not the familiar sound of a dog or a coyote. They were too afraid to walk the short distance home, and so Jolene had to give them a ride home in her car, ONLY 1½ BLOCKS AWAY!

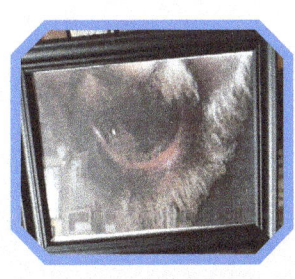

Morgan, Jenna & Karissa

Though they have called Garrison home their entire lives, all of the walkers said they had "NEVER heard anything like that guttural growl before…"

 Witnesses of the 'Weird'

Here's what's weird about what we saw.

1. Tree was not broken. It was about 40 feet tall. And about 2-3 feet in diameter.

2. The broken branch was about 12 feet from the ground to the break. It had been twisted about 2 or 3 times around. But, it was still attached. After it was broken, the top of the tree was about 1½ feet from the ground.

3. There were 5 smaller branches that were "shoots" off of the main broken branch. Each "shoot" was approximately 1-1½ inch in diameter.

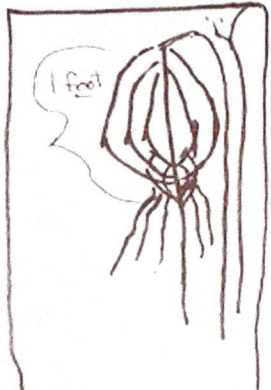

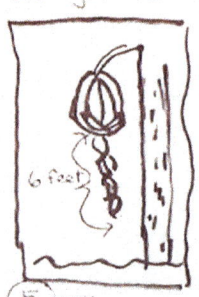

4. The branches were all pulled together, about 1 foot down from where they grew out of the main branch. They were small and green- so they all bent easily without breaking...

5. They were all braided together. About 6 feet.

** There was not one broken branch of any size in the whole park.

6. After they had been braided down about 6 feet, they were all tied together in a large knot.. the ends hung down about 6 inches, and were 2 feet above the ground.

 Witnesses of the 'Weird'

This tree did not look to me like it was wind-broken.

TREE BREAKS

WIND

When wind causes a tree break — it is snapped. Sometimes there are 3 or 4 trees side by side — and they are all snapped in a row. All broken in the same direction. This is wind...

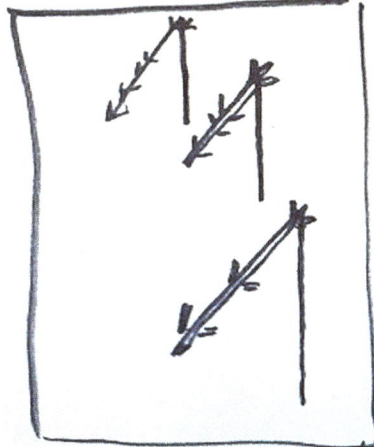

BIG FOOT

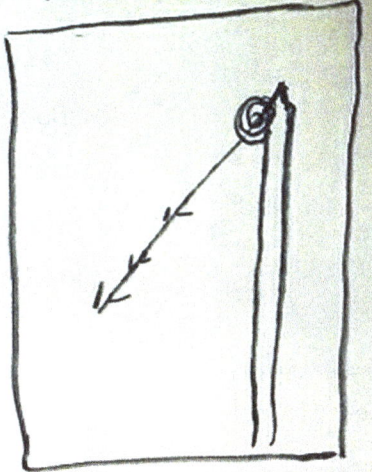

Bark (at the break) is still attached to the tree. It is twisted around (the branch) about 2 or 3 times. It is broken, but still attached... and, it may stay that way for years — This is "WEIRD" — it was definitely not done by the wind.

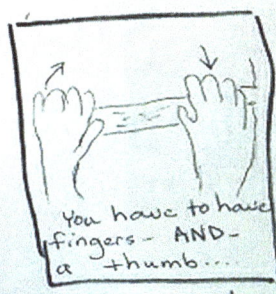

You have to have fingers — AND — a thumb...

Picture hands twisting a bottle cap open... (twisted in opposite ways)

Museum Investigation Team

Since our investigation, our Museum Research Team: Tamara Stier, Art Wach and I, have drawn several opinions as to the now 'famous flag.' I want to include their thoughts in this book since the majority of the investigation has been my own personal undertaking and my own opinions.

Harriett McFeely

Harriett McFeely – "I wonder if we need to change our attitude. We consider this torn, braided and knotted flag an act of vandalism... but do the Bigfoot or whoever or whatever is doing this... do they consider it vandalism????"

Tamara Stier

Tamara Stier – "This mystery had been an adventure! I don't know what happened; however, I believe we should consider all options, being open to ones we don't know yet, and maybe we can find some clues to discover the truth."

Art Wach

Art Wach – "Interesting..."

Museum Investigation Team

Jenna continued to observe 'WEIRD' happenings at their home. She has four round lilac bushes near her deck on the side of her house. Each bush is about four feet in height. On three different occasions, Jenna discovered that her lilac bushes were mashed down as if SOMEONE or SOMETHING had sat on them OR were they looking in their windows?? ONLY WHO???

Jenna's lilac bushes.

Later Jenna found hair stuck between the boards of her front porch deck.

At night, Jenna's dog Ellie, a white Labrador retriever, WILL NOT go outdoors. She looks toward the cemetery through the railings on the porch, BUT SHE WILL NOT LEAVE THE PORCH..., then she goes back into the house...

Janna's white Lab, Ellie.

Museum Investigation Team

THE COLUMBUS TELEGRAM — LOCAL — FRIDAY, AUGUST 28, 2020 · A3

Woman claims Bigfoot tore American flag

McFeely investigates Garrison Cemetery event

HANNAH SCHRODT
The Columbus Telegram

The mystery behind an American flag being torn and braided over Memorial Day weekend in the Garrison Cemetery has been thought to be the victim of extreme storms or possible flag desecration. But one theory that's been gaining traction is stranger than the normal explanations.

According to Harriet McFeely, the tattering and braiding of the flag is the evidence of an animal that most don't believe even exist - Bigfoot.

McFeely stopped by the Hruska Memorial Public Library in David City last week to examine the flag. A life-long believer of the creature, she owns Nebraska Bigfoot Crossroads of America, a museum and research center in Hastings dedicated to the Sasquatch.

The subject of the torn flag had been brought up during David City's Flag Day ceremony. Jim Daro, Legion commander, and other veterans displayed the destroyed flag, though it had been too windy that day to retire any of the flags.

That may have, in fact, been a blessing to McFeely as the flag would have been properly burned if not for the unfavorable weather.

McFeely heard of the story after The Banner published an article about the torn American flag in its June 18 edition. She then visited the Garrison Cemetery and David City area to conduct research.

The proof that it's the work of Bigfoot, McFeely explained, is the braiding and little knots that can be seen on the flag.

"If you look right here, there's a knot. A perfect knot right there," McFeely pointed out last week. "They tie the knots with their fingers."

When asked about how a supposedly large creature like Bigfoot could make small knots, McFeely noted that it's a habit picked up by the creatures' early years.

"There are two things to think about. First of all, they have kids and guess how big their fingers are when kids - they're littler than mine," McFeely said. "I know some men that crochet. If you learned that when you were 7-years-old, it wouldn't matter if you're your size or bigger. Once you learn how to do that,

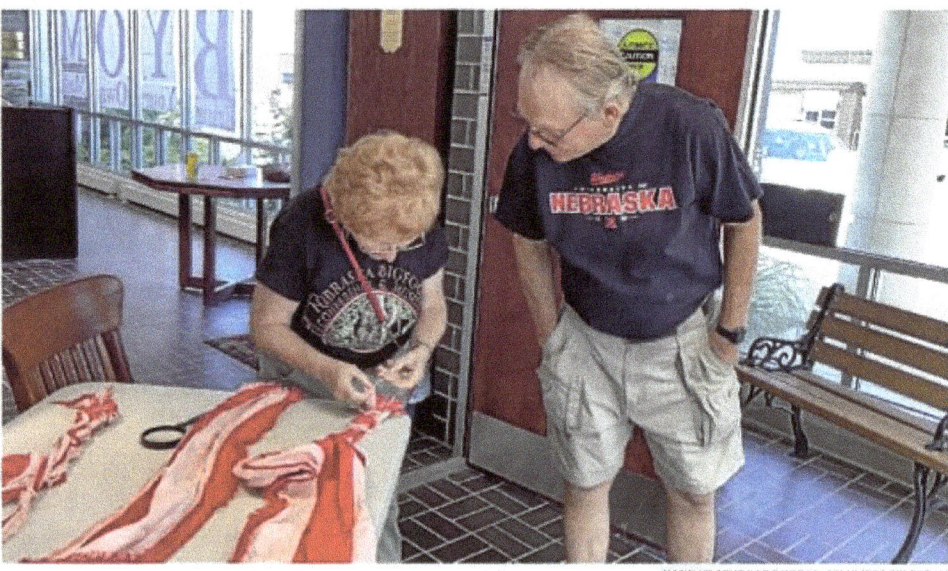

HANNAH SCHRODT PHOTOS, COLUMBUS TELEGRAM
Harriet McFeely, left, and Jim Daro examine a torn and braided American flag, which McFeely believes to be the work of Bigfoot.

WATCH NOW
Visit ColumbusTelegram.com to watch a video of Harriet McFeely explaining the evidence surrounding an American flag being torn and braided by Bigfoot.

Pictured is a torn and braided American flag as seen last week. Previously thought to be the work of extreme weather/misplaced intentions or of flag desecration, Harriet McFeely, owner of the Bigfoot Crossroads of America museum in Hastings, believes the flag to be evidence of Bigfoot.

you know how to do it."

The American flag in question actually belonged to Daro's family.

"My Uncle George donated it to the cemetery 29 years ago," Daro said, noting that for the past almost three decades, the flag had been displayed twice a year at Garrison Cemetery on Veteran's Day and Memorial Day.

The flag has since been donated to McFeely for her museum.

McFeely added that Bigfoot also leaves behind evidence of braiding horses' manes.

"There's some lady that lives on a farm... And she's got two horses that come in all the time. It was, she didn't even know that, but about a week before she came (to the museum), which is about two weeks ago now, the night before and the horse had just come in and it was braided. And she said it's often (it happens)," McFeely shared.

That's just one of several stories McFeely has heard in regards to strange stories in this region.

"(One lady) went to check on her lamb, or she had the edge because it was hot weather, just wanted to make sure they were OK," she said. "They had water (but) she couldn't find one. And she looked and looked. Finally, on the third time, she found it — something had taken a hold of its back leg and pull the clear out of the socket and pulled the whole leg. It was gone."

It had been pointed out to McFeely that another animal such as a mountain lion could have gotten to the lamb. After consulting with someone who knows about wild animals, though, McFeely said her mind couldn't be swayed.

"Either a mountain lion or a bear, depending on where you live, when they do something like that they take their claws, and they pull it off. This had no marks on it at all... she said she never ever did find the leg. So who knows where it is?" she said.

Other cultures have different names for the Bigfoot, such as those in Tibet and the Himalayans who refer to the creature as the Yeti, she added.

Having always enjoyed outside activities such as exploring and hiking, McFeely's obsession began in May 1953 when Edmund Hillary became one of the first people to climb to the top of Mt. Everest.

"As he was going up the mountain, the snow was deep and right there in front of him were huge footprints...," she said. "They laid a pickax right next to the footprints to show how long they were and I would guess they were 18 inches long at least."

McFeely took possession of the torn American flag last Thursday. There will be a private celebration for the flag's entry into the Nebraska Bigfoot Crossroads of America on Sept. 15. The rest of the week, though, anyone who resides and Garrison and visits the museum can gain free admission.

"I can't explain it. That's all I'll say," Daro said. "I've never seen a Bigfoot. I've never seen the tracks. But, I mean, that's probably as good as explanation as any."

Hannah Schrodt is the news editor of The Columbus Telegram. Reach her via email at hannah.schrodt@lee.net.

Hannah Schrodt, The Columbus Telegram, Columbus, Nebraska, August 28, 2020, used by permission. Columbus Telegram online, https://www.newspapers.com/newspage/677983546/ Accessed April 7, 2021.

Disclaimer:

I do not say as a fact that a BIGFOOT destroyed the Garrison, Nebraska flag...

I do believe, however, that there is a great deal of evidence that points in this direction.

All around the world, many horses have had their hair braided by some mysterious happening...their manes are not dirty or dusty. They have no weeds, stickers, or straw in their manes. The braids are very intricate, and they contain loops and a tight knot at the end. (Similar to the braids on the flag!)

An the following pages of this book, I have included many pictures of braided horses from Russia, Siberia, Australia, and other countries, plus pictures from Nebraska, Colorado, and Montana.

In my opinion, these braids WERE NOT caused by wind, weather, other horses, or rolling on their backs.

Also— I DEFINITELY DO NOT BELIEVE that the flag in Garrison was damaged OVERNIGHT by wind, extreme weather, or vandalism.

In addition to the many pictures, I have had experts from Nebraska, Montana, Kansas, Oregon, Texas and Russia review the facts and evidence. Each one has voiced their opinion, and NONE BELIEVE this extreme damage was caused by weather...

So, I have endeavored to give all of the currently available evidence.

My question: If not Bigfoot, then WHO? WHAT? WHY?? And, what evidence is there???

I have presented my case, and I urge each reader to come to their own conclusions, and to do their own thorough, painstaking, complete research, and overlooking no detail, AND, WITH AN OPEN MIND!

Harriett McFeely

Museum Investigation Team

Needless to say, my mind was racing! And, there are many crucial points that we all agreed upon:

1. I felt the flag was deliberately braided. As Igor Burtsev said, "In my opinion: such is there Bigfoot pranks, to plait the strips of the flags into the braids."

2. In my opinion the flags condition had nothing to do with the weather or high winds. I have NEVER seen the wind make a perfect braid or twirl, and then put a single red string around it and tie a small, tight knot.

  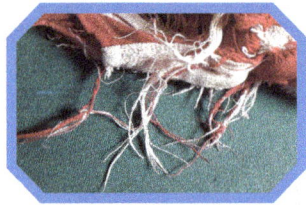

3. The braids are nothing new to me. I have seen many exactly like them featured in Don Monroe's exhibit in my BIGFOOT MUSEUM in Hastings, Nebraska.

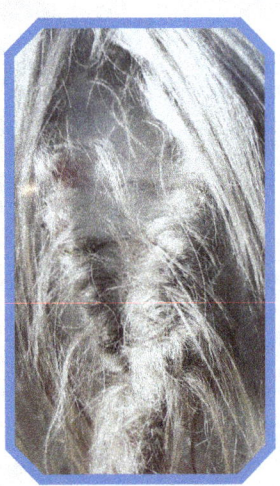  

4. Similar braids can be seen in photographs of multiple horses whose manes were "mysteriously" braided with knots and loops from all over the WORLD.

5. In addition, I have many pieces of actual horse hair that has been braided by unknown sources, so, who or what did the braiding??

 Museum Investigation Team

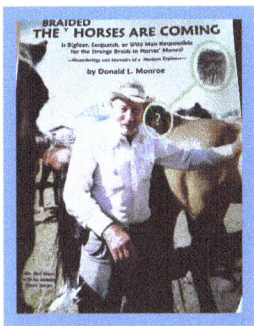

6. The extensive braided horse hair exhibit was donated to the BIGFOOT MUSEUM by Mr. Don Monroe, of Montana. Don has been a RESEARCHER and EXPLORER for over 60 years, and he has done a tremendous job documenting the BRAIDED HORSES!!

Typical Nebraska tree breaks.

7. The light, reddish brown hair that was found on the front and back of the flag, by a museum researcher who has over 30 years' experience is VERY intriguing. I could find no cats, dogs or other animals with hair that color who may have contributed to the mystery hairs. In the future he hopes to complete the DNA testing.

Garrison tree break.

8. The braided tree limb that was found in the park is VERY difficult to dismiss. There are several examples of tree breaks on exhibit in the MUSEUM from photos taken in Nebraska, Colorado, Washington, Oregon, California, Kansas and other states. HOWEVER, I have NEVER seen the branches braided together like the ones that were seen in the Garrison Park incident…

Museum Investigation Team

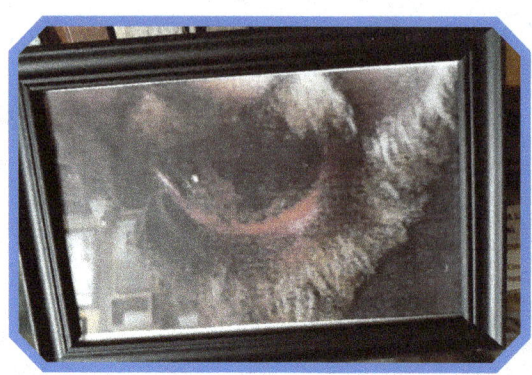

9. Another striking piece of evidence was the HORRIFIC SCREAM heard by the 'walkers'. Such sounds are well documented in areas where BIGFOOT ACTIVITY has been observed.

10. More evidence was collected during a follow-up visit to the cemetery and during additional interviews with witnesses. Behind the cemetery runs Keran Creek, which connects with the 'WEIRD' and all of its tributaries that travel all over central Nebraska, including the Little Blue River. There have been many sightings and 'WEIRD' happenings that have occurred across this area for 100s of years.

 # The Horses and the Flag

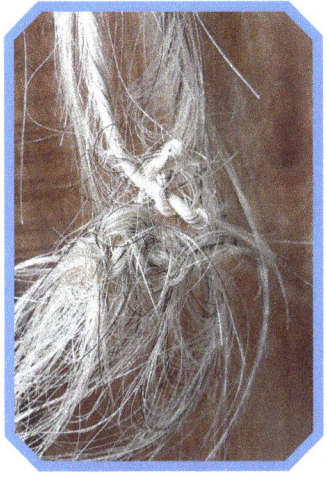
Braided Horse's Mane

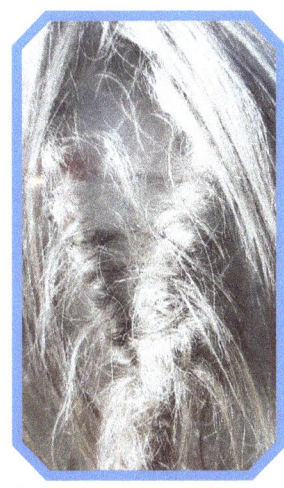
Braided Horse's Mane

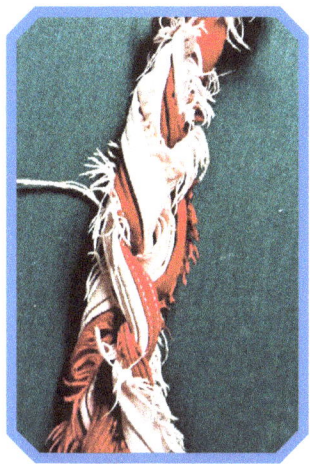
Red & White Braided Together

Small hands, Small braids...

 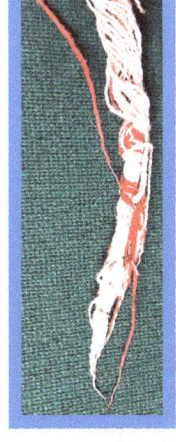  

Small Braids in Garrison flag.

 The Horses and the Flag

*Large hands,
Large braids...*

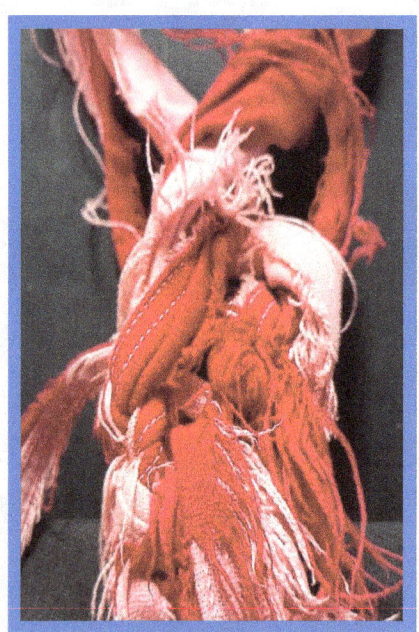

Large Knot in
Garrison flag.

Braided Horse's
Mane

Red and White rope
intricately tied.
Found in a barn.

The Experts

One Researcher said:

If something is
WEIRD,

chances are it's
WEIRD,

and
Our Experts Said:

1. Mr. Don Monroe, The Braided Horses are Coming
2. Dr. Igor Burtsev, Catching Up with Bigfoot: Kuzbass (Siberia) and Beyond
3. Mr. Jim Myers, The Sasquatch Outpost
4. Mr. Richard Soule, Hominologist
5. Mr. Scott Barta, Sasquatch Investigation of the Rockies (S.I.R)
6. Mr. Ron Morehead, Sierra Sounds, Quantum Bigfoot
7. Mr. Joe Taylor, Mt. Blanco Fossil Museum
8. Mr. M. K. Davis, Bigfoot Researcher, The Davis Report

The Experts

Horse breeder Neil Hinck, on whose ranch numerous braids were found, portrayed on the cover of Don Monroe's book.

Mr. Don Monroe

For the 50 white stars on the blue background. The following evidence of this book speaks for itself over the following pages.

Until recently, I have had many opportunities to explore caves, great wilderness areas and the supernatural or the 'macabre.' However, since a child, I know in my heart there were likely spirits and ghosts to concern with, BUT I have mostly disregarded efforts to explore them, not to say this is done by ghosts, BUT after 60 years, I have gone about everywhere and rationalized almost anything. Therefore, I conclude nearly everything is TRUE. As this book has explained, everything is done in such a strange manner that opens the doors beyond imagination to what is possible and unexplained… The flag destruction is exactly what it was — it was DESTRUCTION.

Let me invite you to join Harriett's Museum crew and closely examine all of the hidden clues to the unknown world. Harriett's research defies imagination…. It is an irreplaceable phenomenon!!

I invite legal scientists and scholars to contemplate this MYSTERY!

For further information, I suggest you may want to pick up a copy of my book,

"The Braided Horses are Coming".

Don Monroe

Don Monroe
Research/Explorer and Author

 # Dr. Igor Burtsev

To Harriett McFeely
with the best wishes
Igor Burtsev

Dr. Igor Burtsev

These pictures are for Harriett.

I am sending you some pictures of braids in manes, you to have imagination, how they plait them. First, I need to tell that they start to plait the laces not from their beginning (bases), but from the ends of laces, making a small net of three or four laces and putting that knot into gaps between laces – upper and upper to the neck, and stopping, when it is difficult to put the knot into the gap between laces.

The humans do by the opposite manner, they start to plait from the bases of hairs (laces) and plaiting to the ends of them.

Several photos attached. I studied this phenomenon in many places, including U.S.A. and Canada, not only on MJK location and Azerbaijan and our side.

The important is that you have found hairs, it's necessary to analyze them as minimum with microscope if you don't have opportunity to study the DNA.

My opinion: such is their (BF's) pranks, to plait the strips of the flag into the braids!

Good Luck,

Igor Burtsev

Igor Burtsev, Ph.D., History

Anthropologist, Author

Moscow, Russia

Dr. Igor Burtsev

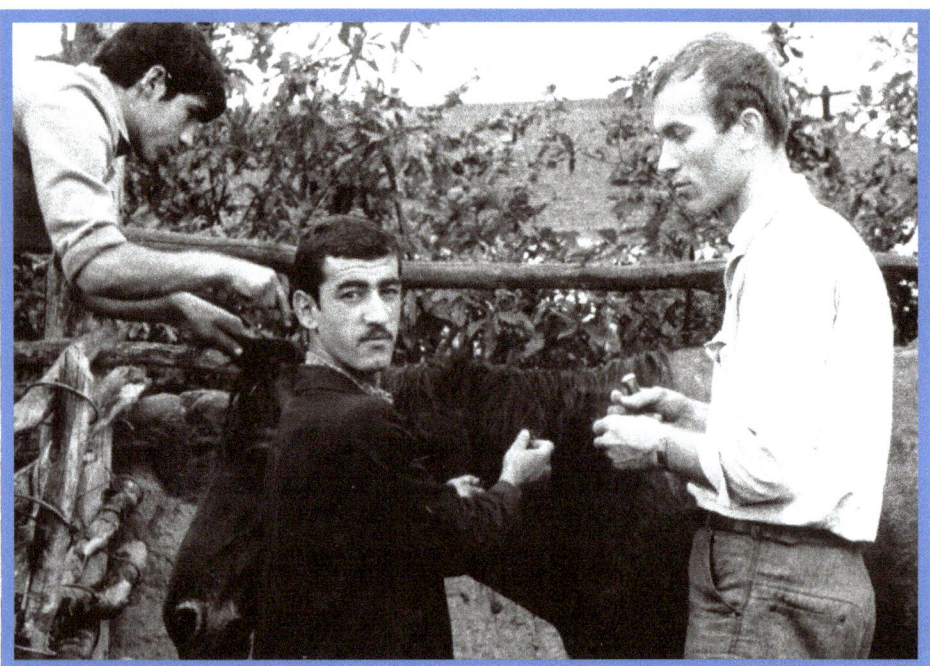

Igor's first expedition was in 1965 in the Caucasus Region to investigate the weaving of horses' hair.

Photographs courtesy of Igor Burtsev, used by permission.

 Dr. Igor Burtsev

1970 - 1975

In the Talysh location in Azerbaijan.

Photographs courtesy of Igor Burtsev, used by permission.

Dr. Igor Burtsev

1970 - 1975
In the Talysh location in Azerbaijan.

Image courtesy of Igor Burtsev, used by permission.

Dr. Igor Burtsev

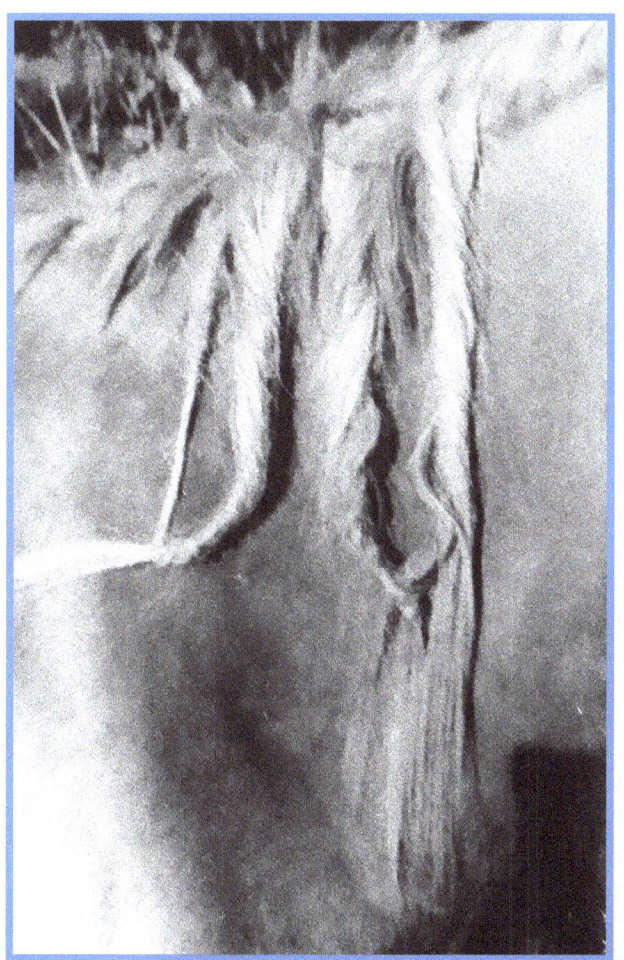

1970 - 1975 In the Talysh location in Azerbaijan.

Photographs courtesy of Igor Burtsev, used by permission.

 # Dr. Igor Burtsev

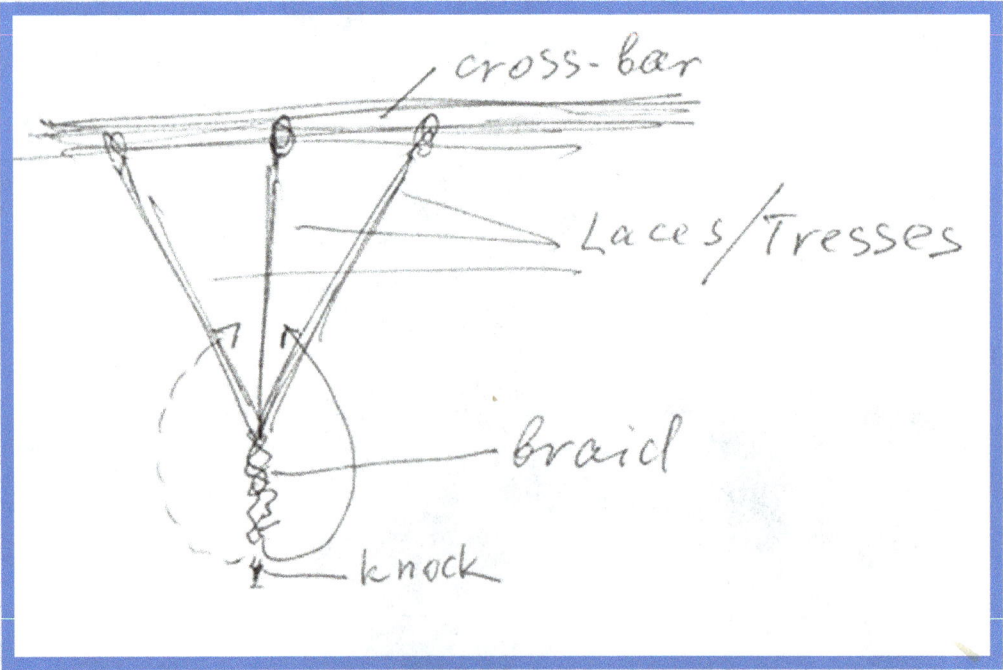

Images courtesy of Igor Burtsev, used by permission.

The Braided Horses – Australia

Australia

There were many major bush fires in Australia in the spring of 2020. Horses and many other animals traveled many miles to escape the fires.

The wild horses in the outback are called BRUMBIES. The only noticeable injuries they sustained were their noses had been singed.

Oh yes, and their manes had been braided!

 The Braided Horses - Australia

The Braided Horses Are Coming... To the United States

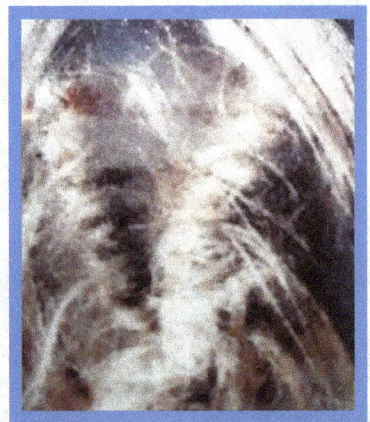
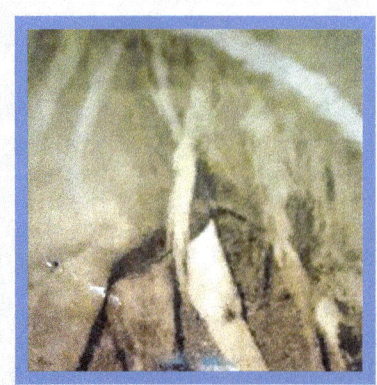

Montana
Horses are knotted anywhere – sometimes in the
pen, sometimes in the pastures.

Braided Horses – USA

The Braided Horses Are Coming... To the United States

South Dakota

Crow Creek Sioux

Braided Horses - USA

The Sasquatch Outpost

I've heard about this phenomenon of horse man braiding, and I've seen horses' manes with intricate braids from all over the country.

Well, last Sunday my friends Paul and Crystal brought their two horses out to South Park... and low and behold, Hunter's mane was braided!! It was clearly an intricate double braid - and was braided by hand.

The question is: who goes out at night and braids these horses' manes? Sasquatch? No matter where they're braided in the country, it's almost always two braids going into a single braid - just like you see on Hunter.

Always two braids into a single braid. I can understand tangling their manes into a mess from activities of throwing their heads, rolling, fighting one another; BUT, always tangling them into 2 braids combining into one at the bottom? Doesn't seem possible to me.

How can you be sure that it's not a Bigfoot unless you're watching your horse constantly to see when their mane becomes knotted in that way?

Jim Myers

Jim Myers

The Sasquatch Outpost

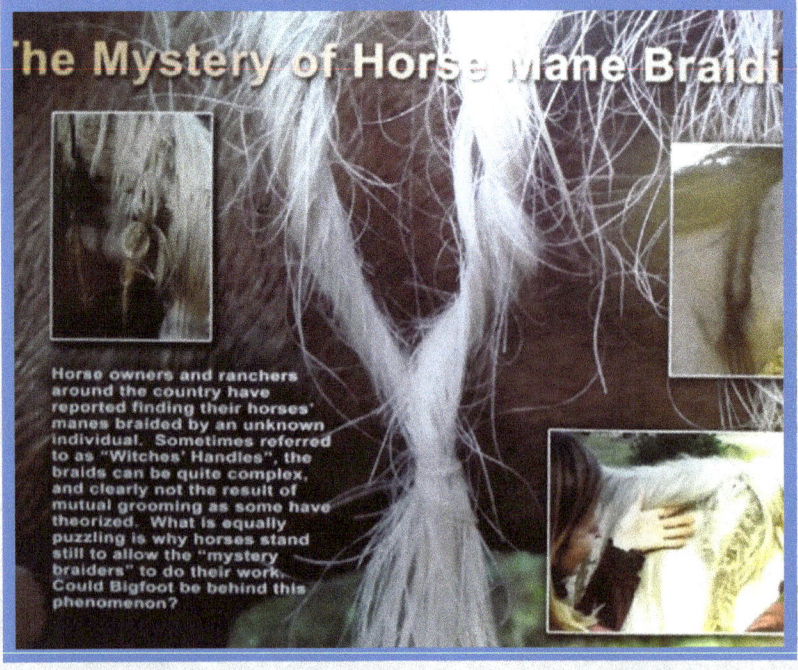

 Braided Horses - Missouri

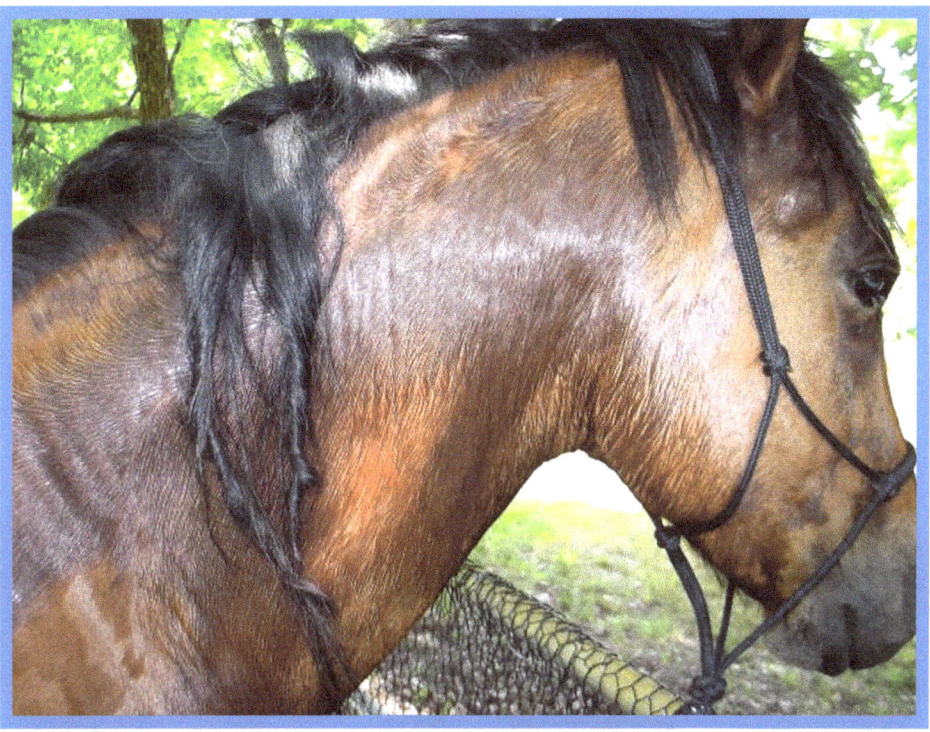

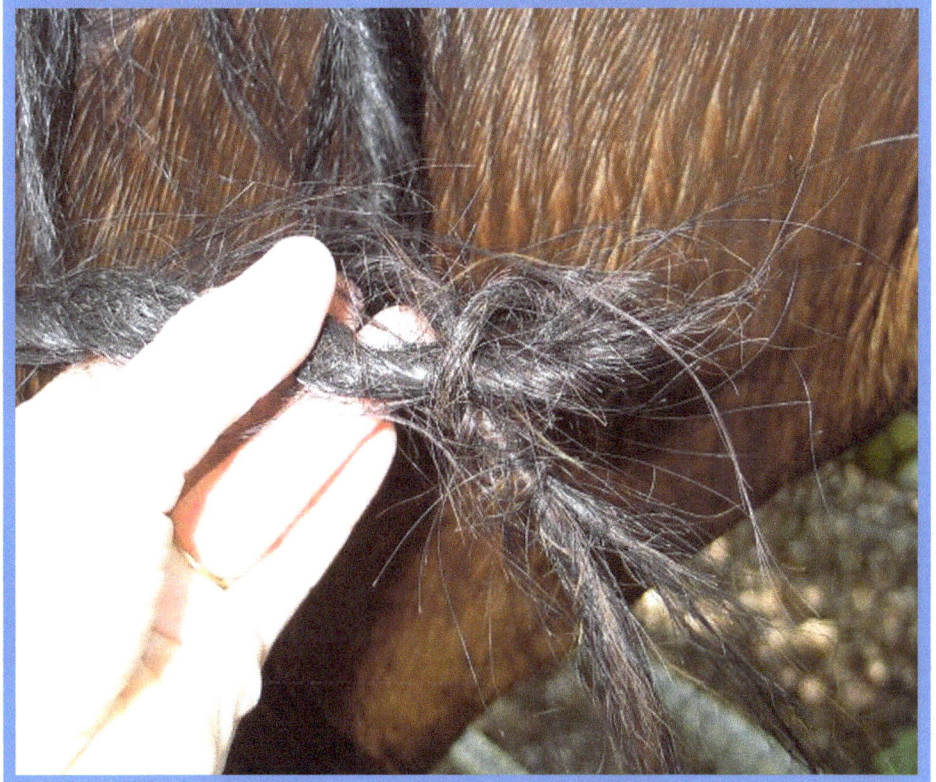

Taken near Joplin, Missouri in 2005-2006.
The owner of the horse keeps her anonymity.

 Braided Horses - Missouri

Taken near Joplin, Missouri, in 2005-2006.
The name of this horse is Miss Sophia.
The owner of the horse keeps her anonymity.
Igor advised her to put a colored ribbon on the horse's neck,
and later it was woven into the braid.

 Braided Horses - Missouri

Taken near Joplin, Missouri, in 2005-2006.
The owner of the horse keeps her anonymity.

 Braided Horses - Missouri

Taken near Joplin, Missouri, in 2005-2006.
The owner of the horse keeps her anonymity.

 Braided Horses - Missouri

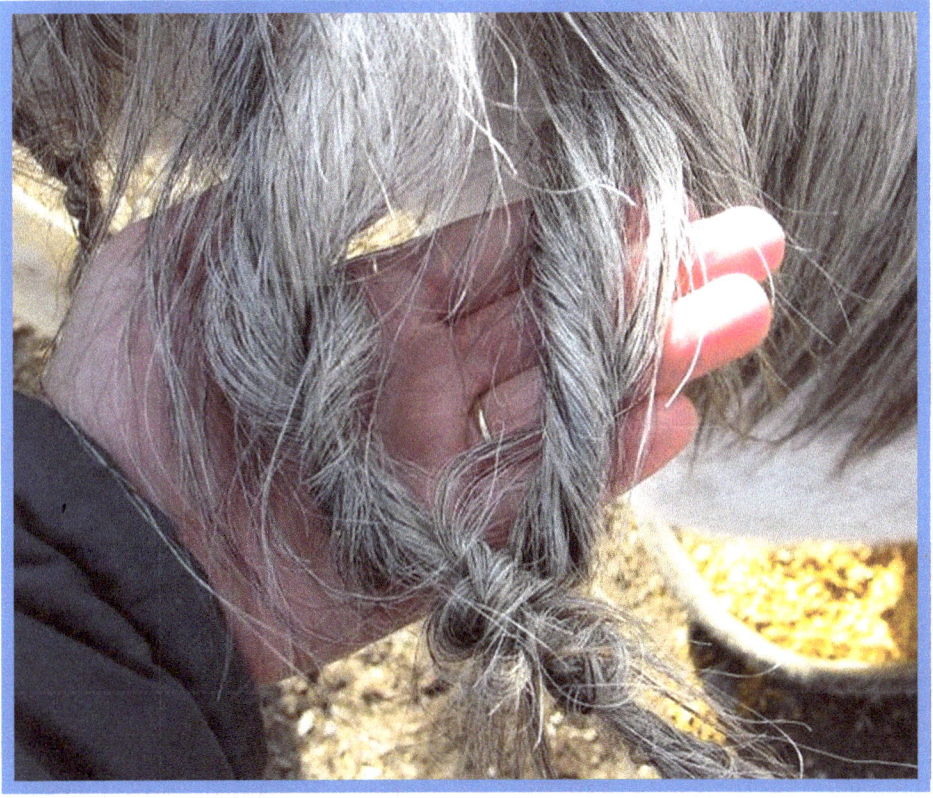

Taken near Joplin, Missouri, in 2005-2006.
The owner of the horse keeps her anonymity.

Braided Horses - Nebraska

The Braided Horses Are Coming... To Nebraska

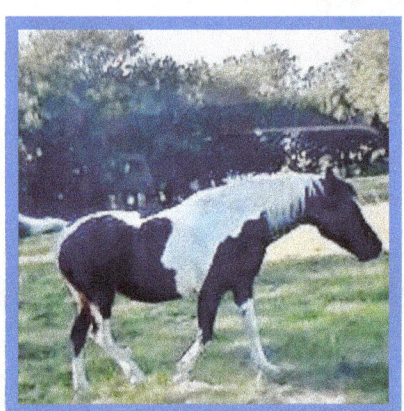

North Bend
"Snap" is a female Pinto.

Her mane has been braided occasionally for over 9 years! She has lived on this farm the entire time. Notice that THE PLATTE RIVER IS BEHIND HER.

"Macy"

Macy is a Native American Reservation in northeastern Nebraska near the Missouri River. They are members of the Iowa tribe. This horse is an oddity: it is a male, not a female, and his tail is braided not his mane. Horses are knotted anywhere – sometimes in the pen, sometimes in the pastures.

Braided Horses - Nebraska

The Braided Horses Are Coming... To Nebraska

"Sweetheart"
Sweetheart is a Quarter Horse.

"Lady"
Lady is a Shetland pony.

Sweetheart and Lady are both mares. They live about 5 miles outside of Hastings, Nebraska. Both horses had spent time in the night out in the pasture and came into the corral in the morning to the stock tank for water. This occurred in January 2020. They have NEVER had their hair braided before or since.

 # Mr. Richard Soule

Consternation in Garrison Nebraska

    There are notable aspects to this study that have paralleled other encounters with Sasquatch/Hominoid activity. I have heard, passed on stories in this region that give credibility to the occurrences that took place Memorial Day weekend in Garrison. To the North of Garrison is David City, NE. A woman I worked with confided to me that her father, a farmer near David City, had long shared a story with his family that he had seen a bear while hunting. This had occurred years before this incident. The farmer was laughed at and was not taken seriously. The woman who shared the story with me said her father was not one to make up a story and stood by his sighting but family members did not believe him.

Mr. Richard Soule

Consternation in Garrison Nebraska

There are no bears in Nebraska and this region is far from any bordering states that do have bear. I told my colleague that I think he saw a Sasquatch and not a bear at all. The farmer has since passed on but I came to this conclusion because the Platte River is a prime location for these hominoids and it was within the range of a Sasquatch to travel.

The second corroborating story took place to the south of Garrison in another County. I believe it was in the 90's that this was reported to a BFRO investigator and later shared with me. A report was never officially made, but I remember these details as they always come to play in some unforeseen future such as this. A well respected and reliable citizen had a sighting of a Bigfoot. Apparently, it was disturbing enough to him that he reported to the BRFO. I don't recall the details, but it was enough of a visual that he was certain it was a Bigfoot.

Back to Garrison and the Flag incident. Garrison lies in between these seemingly unconnected accounts of hominoid activity. Given the location, the community seems to be a likely hotbed of activity. There are significant sources of water; reservoirs are strewn throughout the farmland. Attached Frame #1 is a map of karst systems nationally that are associated with caves and underground natural springs.

Mr. Richard Soule

Consternation in Garrison Nebraska

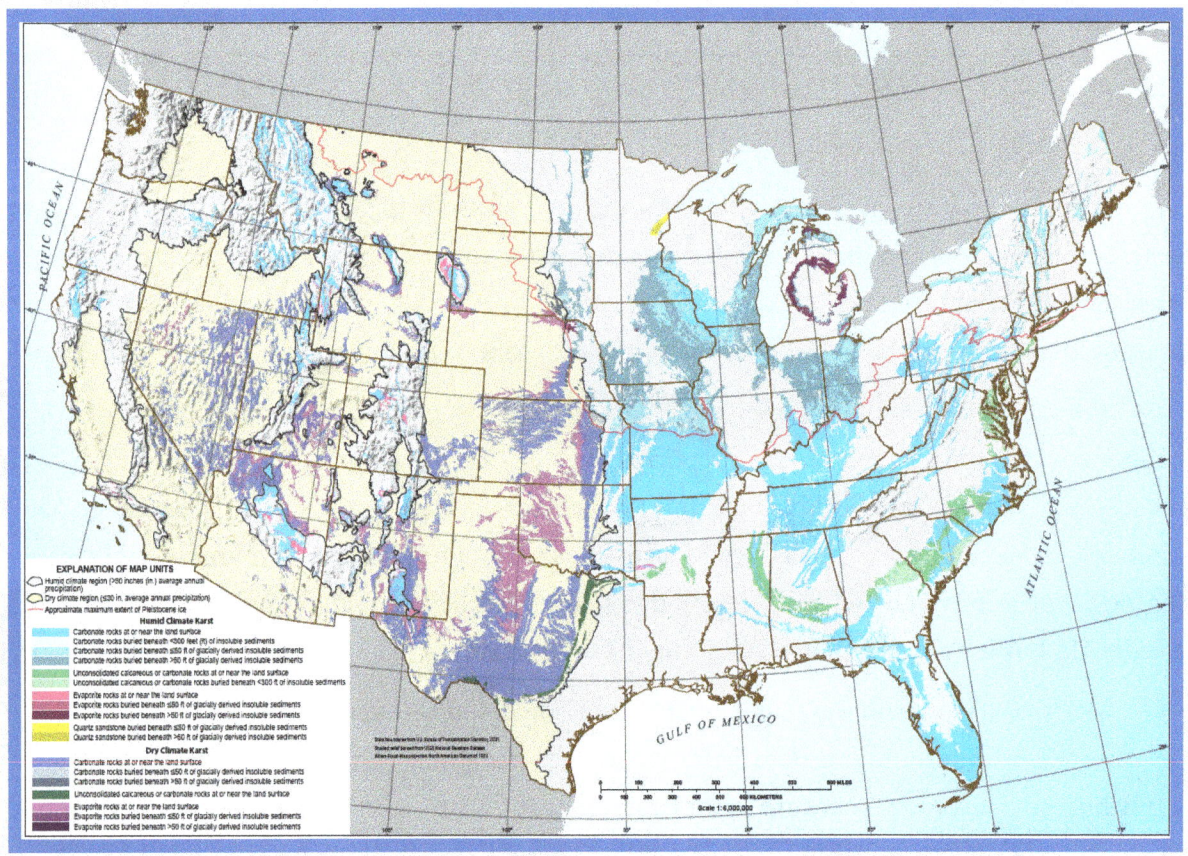

Frame #1: U.S. Karst Map: Karst and potential karst areas in soluble rocks in the contiguous United States.

Mr. Richard Soule

Consternation in Garrison Nebraska

Frame #2: Karst In Nebraska

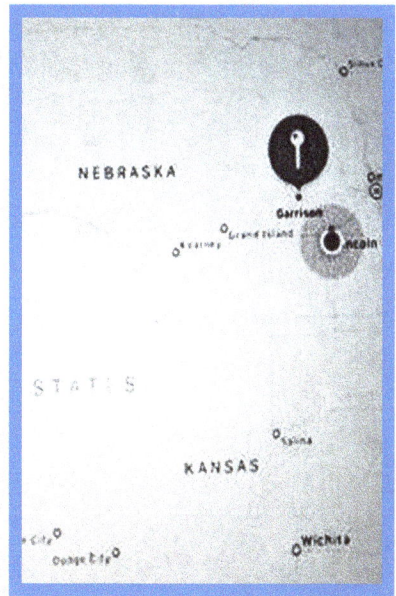

Frame #3: Location of Garrison Cemetery

Mr. Richard Soule

Consternation in Garrison Nebraska

Frame #2 is a map of karst in Nebraska and Garrison appears to be within this habitat that I know are favorable to these hominoids. The natural springs offer fresh water and the caves created by these karst systems of underground water are ideal for hominoids.

Map frame #3 is of the Garrison Cemetery. Cemeteries have a long history associated with hominoid activity. This does not surprise me to hear the experiences near the cemetery especially if a chicken is placed near the creek. That would draw in other wildlife and an opportunistic Sasquatch would stop by this location to see if there are any easy calories.

The village of Garrison, only comprising of some fifty people would be fairly predictable for a Sasquatch to move through at night. Peek in windows, like the incident of the flattened bushes, and riffle through the garbage perhaps at the park. Hence the growls at people interfering in the snack search. When you put this all together if forms a picture of hominoid activity that parallel many of the experiences reported around the world.

The flag debasing may be the clincher in how all this fits together. Having raised the flag and leaving it an extra day may not seem out of the ordinary for the humans involved with this story. The local Sasquatch may have taken issue to the normal predictability in a routine that is rarely altered. The flag hanging just more day perhaps raised the ire of the hominoid, not knowing when it would be retrieved, and the people would go away. Tearing it out of frustration and then braiding it in repair is a way to pass the time and encourage the flag to go away along with the people who come to look at it.

Patriotic or passive aggressive, the braiding of the flag is a sign of hominoid activity documented globally. The hairs left behind are the smoking gun if they can be tested. A DNA test resulting in 99% Homo sapiens 1% unknown would be good enough for me to rank this as a Heartland Hominoid!

Richard Soule

Richard Soule

Hominologist

August, MMXX

Mr. Scott Barta

On July 26th 2020, my good friend, SIR member and head of The Bigfoot Crossroads of America Museum and Research Center, Harriett McFeely called me to discuss a series of events that had happened in the small town of Garrison, Nebraska population of 54 souls. The next day she sent me numerous photographs of an American flag that had so many anomalies both on the flag and events surrounding the flag. Harriett is a stickler for details and always asked additional follow-up questions that most people would not think to ask. When I saw the pictures, I was astonished. Now, back in February 2019, I first met Don Monroe. He did a presentation of horses on his ranch that would come in from his pastures with braided manes that he attributed to Sasquatch in the area. He showed me several examples, each very unique in detail of this braided horse hair. I couldn't help but see a possible correlation of the intricacy of both the flag and horse manes. Don and Harriett have had much more in depth conversations about the mannerisms of the horses after they would come back and Don would discover these braids. Several things Don pointed out were first that the horses did not eat initially, and second was that the horses would keep the braided side away from view.

After several days they would be starving and ready to eat. I personally, have seen horseshoe rabbits and elk behave very oddly when I am having experiences in the forest. Not like 'camp deer' behavior which is easy to observe after several nights in the woods. This behavior is much more profound where the animals seem confused and out of sorts. The flag is like nothing I have ever seen no matter what the age, condition, amount of use or situation a flag has been through. This flag could never have gone from used twice a year within the colors vibrant and in fantastic condition to methodically shredded, weaved, wrapped in a tennis ball sized knot overnight. Vandalism is out of the question in my mind. Way too much energy to create the situation this flag is in over the course of an evening. This American icon would take humans days under sterile conditions to manifest. A storm may twist and rip a worn out flag which had seen better days but it still would not create so many unique features in my opinion.

Mr. Scott Barta

So, with the chronology of the townspeople who remember the flag throughout the years always in tip top condition and more in particular the days leading up to how it was found, it simply defies a logical answer. This American flag holds secrets and possible answers to something greater than weather, vandals or just wear and tear. We may never unlock those secrets or get the answers that will suit everyone who gazes upon this American flag. None of that matters; what matters is the American flag, which symbolizes so many different ideas but represents all Americans and American ideals in general. This American flag symbolizes the independence to see what it has been through and the freedom of each individually to determine for themselves what that means.

Respectfully,

Scott F. Barta

Scott F. Barta

Co-Founder, Sasquatch Investigations of the Rockies (S.I.R.)

 # Mr. Ron Morehead

Hi Harriett,

Thanks for allowing me the opportunity to read these accounts.

Weird is certainly an appropriate word for many of these types of unexplained events. If the natural elements, such as the weather, have been ruled out then we must consider something else.

As you know, years ago I began to delve into quantum physics and wrote a book, "The Quantum Bigfoot," and I think it helps us humans to perhaps understand the 'weird' stuff that seems to take place in our world. That book is based on my personal 'weird' experiences with a family of these beings in California that are known as Bigfoot. I figured that there must be a rule or a law in physics that could answer many of the questions that haunted me. I also have a religious background, and I am fairly versed in Biblical scriptures, and in ancient text. If we look closer into the red-letter edition of the Good Book, I think we can understand that Christ worked His miracles using the laws that His father put in place. And, more importantly, He said that we could do the same. I know of no-one who can walk on water yet, so I think we have a ways to go.

 Mr. Ron Morehead

The late Dr. Edgar Mitchell said that it takes classical and quantum sciences together to have clear perception. He also said, "There are no unnatural or supernatural phenomenon, only very large gaps in our knowledge of what is natural…we should strive to fill those gaps of ignorance."

So these mysteries of 'weird' occurrences do not surprise me…nothing surprises me anymore. I think we should all learn to understand that what we see and experience in our three-dimensional environment is not all there is and some things just seem weird.

Again, thanks for allowing me to chime in this story. I hope all is well with you and wish you the very best.

Ron Morehead

Ron Morehead
Producer of *"Sierra Sounds"*
Author of *"Quantum Bigfoot"*

Mr. Joe Taylor

This story, "A Walk on the WEIRD Side," is one of the most compelling stories I've read.

What, or who could do these things to an American flag? Was it a Bigfoot? Weird?

Yes. An excellent read. One hopes that Harriett McFeely will follow up on this story.

Joe Taylor

Joe Taylor
Mt. Blanco Fossil Museum
Crosbyton, Texas

 # Mr. M. K. Davis

In Don Monroe's famous book, *The Braided Horses are Coming*, Don wrote an incredible statement that I have carefully quoted with his permission. Don wrote, "Important Notes on the 1967 Roger Patterson Film!"

In this book segment, M. K. Davis surfaces indisputable film evidence to validate that "wild men actually can manage plaiting!"

"Yeah, and WOW, M. K., what's next??"

"Yeah, Don, I assure you that is true! On the original Roger Paterson film footage, 'Patty' Sasquatch can actually be seen WITHOUT A DOUBT to have braided hair, and much, much more!!"

 # Mr. M. K. Davis

Patty was filmed by Roger Patterson October 20, 1967 at Bluff Creek California.

 # Mr. M. K. Davis

After having examined the Patterson Sasquatch film very closely, there is no doubt that the subject is sporting a braid in her head hair. It can be seen to have a herringbone pattern and to move about the head with her changes in position. To support this I submit these images:

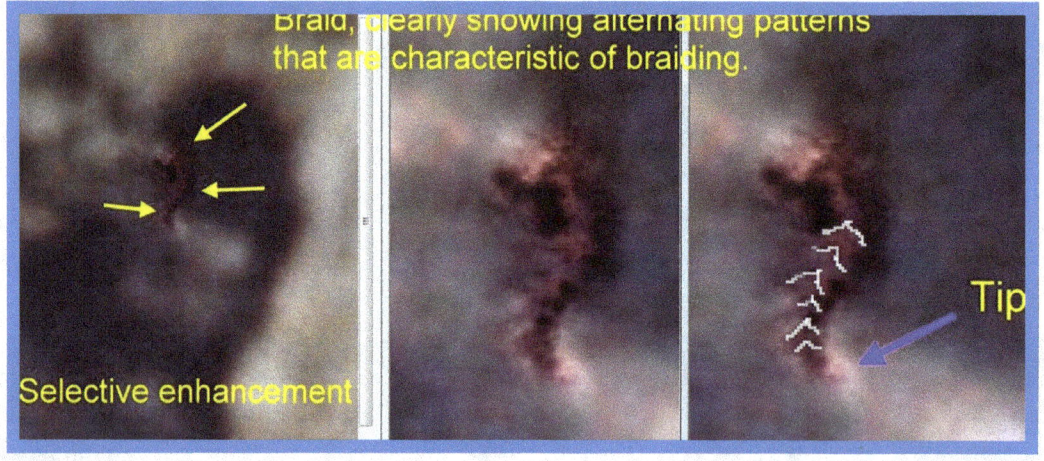

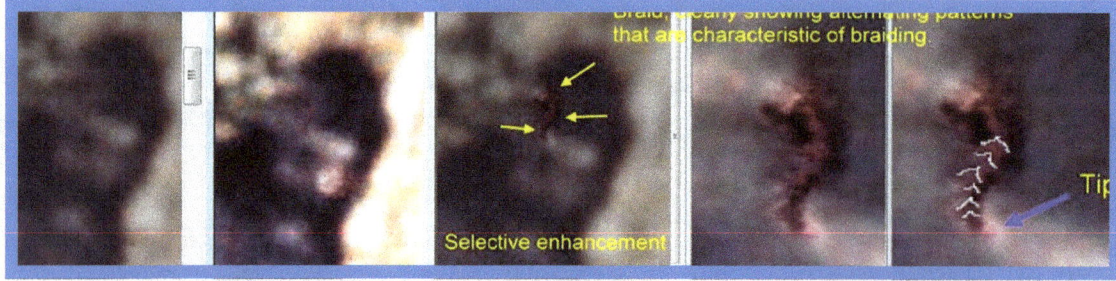

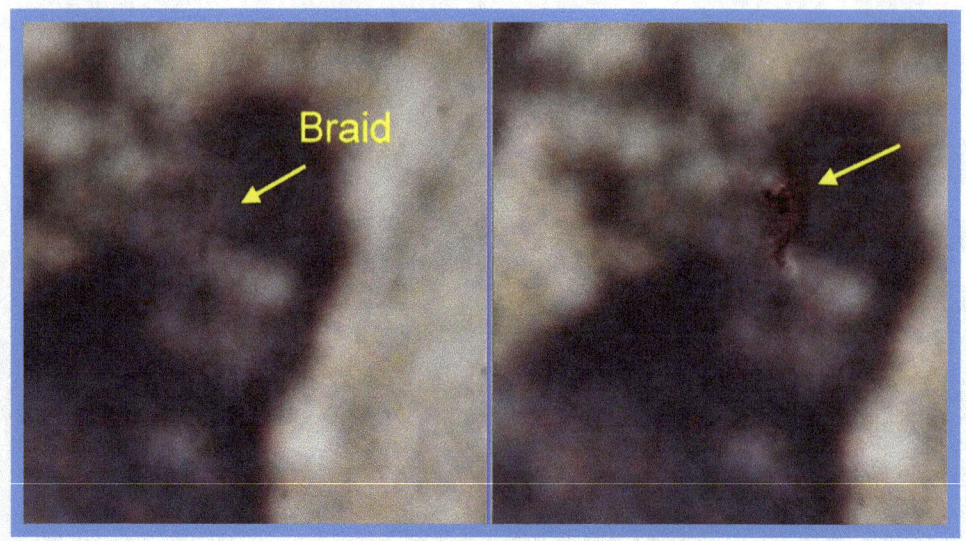

Enhanced images by M. K Davis, used by permission.

Mr. M. K. Davis

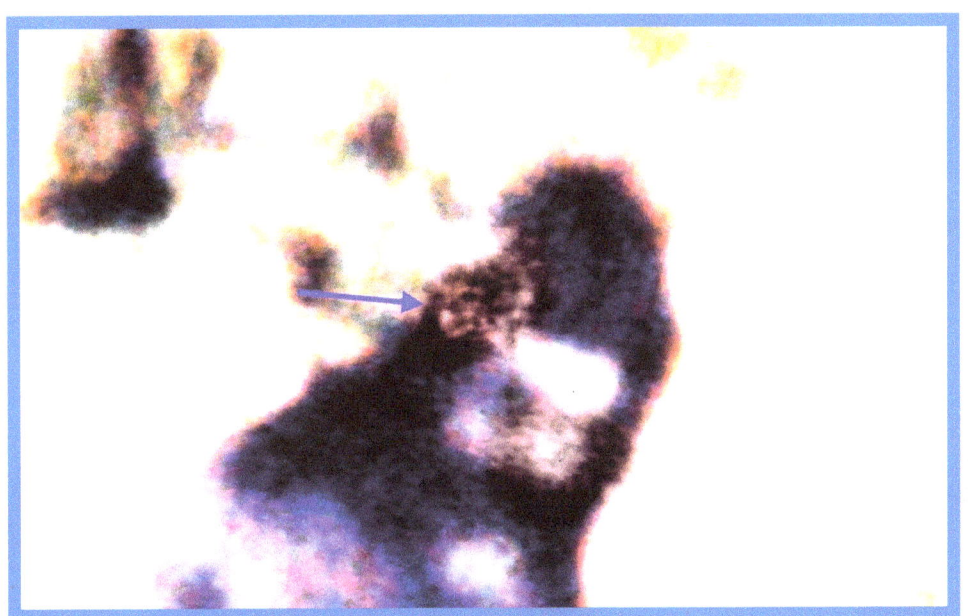

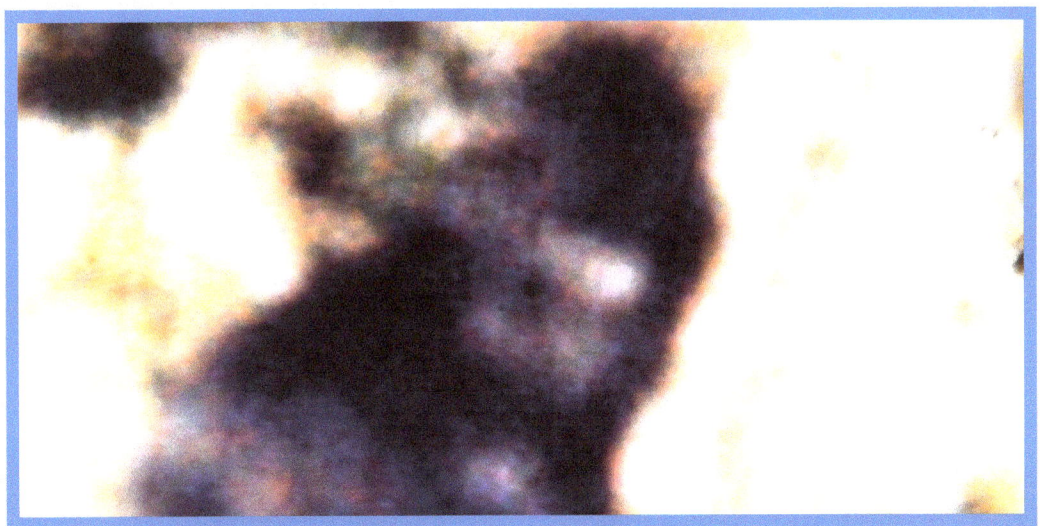

M.K. Davis

M. K. Davis, Bigfoot Researcher

The Davis Report

More Evidence

All of these images of braided hair are from Don Monroe's extensive collection.

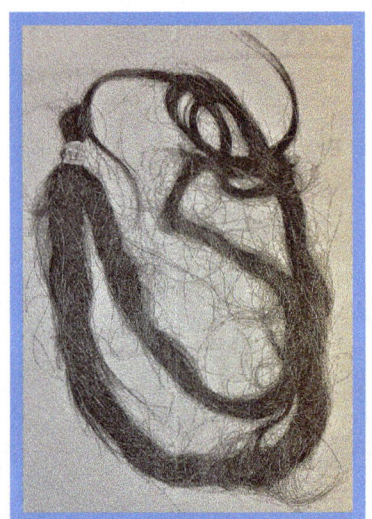

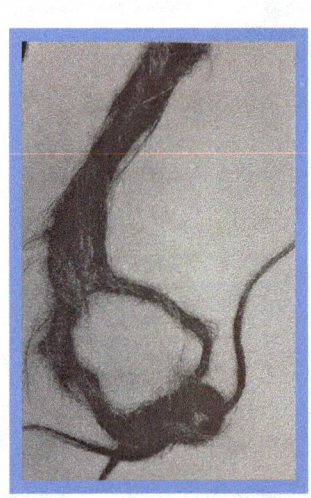
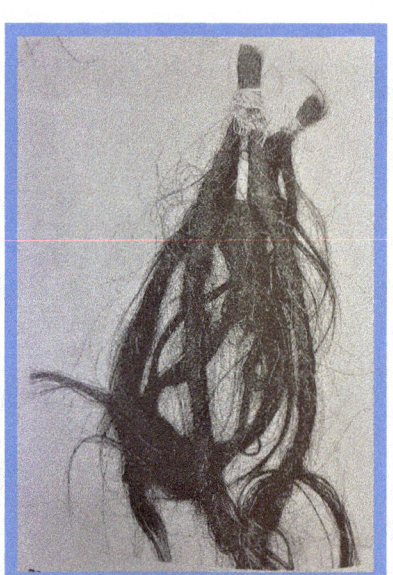

 # More Evidence

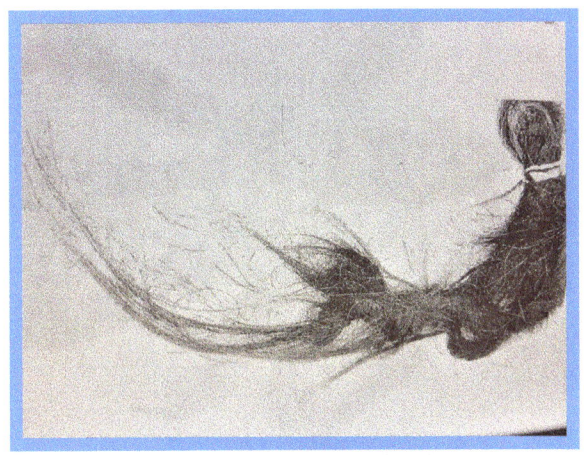

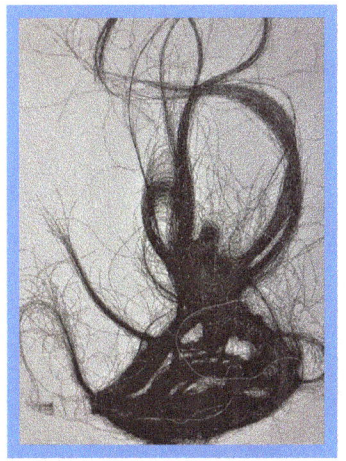

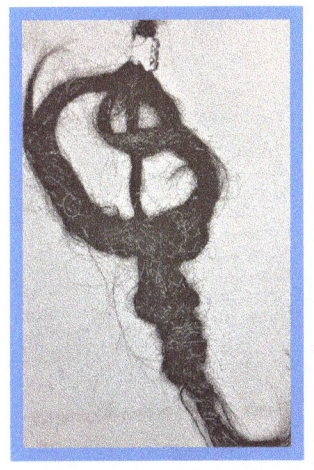

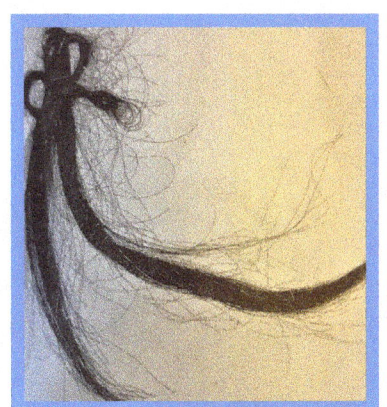

These pictures were all taken, by permission, from Don Monroe's five star (*****) book, **The Braided Horses are Coming!**

Breaking News!
(In the Last 100 Years!)

From a Local Newspaper Columnist[1]

York News-Times

Chatterbaum
Bigfoot and more

By Todd Kirshenbaum Jun 16, 2020 Updated Aug 7, 2020 0

Todd Kirshenbaum

By Todd Kirshenbaum

Last week at work I overheard my co-worker Becca talk about going to a Bigfoot museum in Nebraska.

I was surprised because I thought I had heard of all the quirky museums in the state. I asked for more

---

[1] Todd Kirshenbaum, "Chatterbaum, Bigfoot and more", York News-Times June 16, 2020, Updated August 7, 2020. Accessed April 7, 2021.

Breaking News!
(In the Last 100 Years!)

News-Times

By Todd Kirshenbaum

Last week at work I overheard my co-worker Becca talk about going to a Bigfoot museum in Nebraska.

I was surprised because I thought I had heard of all the quirky museums in the state. I asked for more clarification and she told me that on the weekends, she takes her kids around Nebraska, doing the state's Passport Program. That past weekend she took in the Tri-cities and one of the places on the Passport Program was a museum dedicated to Bigfoot. After doing some digging, I found out she was telling the truth....there was a Bigfoot Museum in Hastings!

Becca told me all about this place which is located across the street from the ballfields in Hastings – it's run by one woman who is Bigfoot expert. I was told she is a delightful woman full of information. I talked to Mr. York Tourism and asked if he had heard of this before. Immediately his eyes grew huge because Bob IS a believer. He grabbed the most current Passport Program brochure and bingo...there it was. So we planned a Saturday trek to go see it.

After a little searching, we found it. It was located in a house. We rang the doorbell and the cutest little woman greeted us. We walked in and got an introduction to the place and to Harriet.

Harriet is an amazing woman. She and her late husband collected an amazing amount of artifacts, mostly from the area. This is where my eyes were opened. I thought there was one alleged Bigfoot but apparently there are dozens of them around the world. We found out they mostly follow a river or creek. I went in a skeptic but after listening to the stories she has heard, I'm convinced there is truth to the story.

She hosts a Bigfoot conference each year, drawing hundreds from all over to mingle with other "Sasquatchers." It's the envy of communities everywhere. She has been invited to take the convention to Omaha, Columbus, Grand Island and other places but since she has gotten a nice grant from the Convention and Visitors Bureau in Hastings for the last few years, I'm guessing she will keep it local.

If you are planning a visit, and I highly recommend it. They are open Mondays-Saturdays, and for a $5 admission, it is well worth it! You'll get a kick out of Harriet too. She is personable, enthusiastic and loaded with information. There are 6-7 rooms in the house with all sorts of exhibits and artifacts. There is also a separate building across the way with plenty of other artifacts. You can wander around or Harriet or a volunteer can answer any questions you may have. I would suggest about an hour to see everything.

Todd Kirshenbaum, "Chatterbaum, Bigfoot and more", York News-Times June 16, 2020, Updated August 7, 2020.

I really appreciate this nice article! Let me correct a few details, though. The museum is actually in a separate addition plus a smaller building, not my house. My husband Dick was very supportive, but the museum was entirely my own project. He never was interested in researching Bigfoot or collecting for the museum, where I had been fascinated since I was 8 years old.

Many thanks, Todd,

Harriett (two t's)

Breaking News!
(In the Last 100 Years!)

COMMENTARY | WHAT ABOUT BOB?

Somethings 'afoot'

Bob Sautter
Director, York
County Visitors
Bureau
mrkcountyvisitors
@gmail.com

Todd mentioned that we made a trip to the Bigfoot Crossroads of America Museum and Research Center in Hastings, which I had heard was there, but had never visited. I did know that there are annual Bigfoot Conventions held in Hastings in the spring of every year. It is the only Bigfoot Museum in the state which makes it very special, but it's also included in the 2020 Nebraska Tourism Passport Program, which makes it even more special. Located at 1205 East 42nd Street off of Highway 281, it's open Tuesday-Saturday 10:30 a.m. - 4:30 p.m. and on Sunday 1 - 4:30 p.m. Admission is $5/person.

Harriett is the owner and operator of this fascinating establishment, and is a virtual fountain of all Bigfoot information. She is a good five inches shorter than me, with unbridled enthusiasm for sharing the historical, educational and scientific research. There's a great story behind each and every object in her collections on display.

I have to admit that I am a "Squatcher" in that I have watched most of the "Hunting Bigfoot" shows, among others, on the History Channel, and I do believe there is something "afoot." There's just too many sightings and incidents to not be true. She was thrilled with my admission. Todd may have been converted.

What I was most surprised at were the number of sightings in Nebraska, all of which were marked by push pins on her Nebraska map. Many pins dotted the southeast and southcentral portions of the state.

A good friend has admitted to seeing one years ago north of York on Highway 81, but has never shared that with anyone for fear of being ridiculed. So, I am not alone in believing!

The other really strange thing that I did not remember seeing or reading about was the braiding of horse's manes and nylon ropes. That seems to be a common occurrence around this area. They believe it to primarily be the work of female "Squatchers," and it's usually done at night when it's dark. Not only does Harriett have pictures, but she has actual manes and ropes on display. The knots on the ropes are not any common types of knots.

Then, there's the story about a flag that was raised in a small town in the vicinity for Memorial Day services.

I'm sure Harriett would love to share the story with you with more details than I can remember. There must be a lot of believers out there as evidenced by the number of visitors in the hour while we were there.

For me, it was the best $5 I've spent in a long time. I want to go back again, and see our new friend Harriett!

Bob Sautter, York News-Times, York, Nebraska, June 24, 2020, used by permission.

Breaking News!
(In the Last 100 Years!)

COMMENTARY | WHAT ABOUT BOB?

There are more "closeted Squatchers" out there than you think

Bob Sautter
Director, York County Visitors Bureau
yorkcountyvisitors
@gmail.com

The response after my last article appeared two weeks ago was fast and furious ... there are more closeted "Squatchers" out there in our area than I could have ever guessed. There have been phone calls and people stopping me on the street. There have been farmers, livestock operators, folks that live in the country, and to my surprise, a former law enforcement person who shared an encounter with one north of Benedict in the same area as one of our readers had reported. They are all respectable folks and well-known in the community, who really haven't shared their story for fear of being labeled crazy and not taken seriously.

You have to admit, whether you are a believer or not, it is still intriguing to know these people who shared with me their experiences in confidence, and that they saw something that defies logical explanation. I also know these people well enough to be certain that they would not make something up to get any attention. After all, in the case of the law enforcement person, it took him almost 30 years to share his story, and that speaks volumes.

I'm pretty sure that Harriett McFeely, The Big Foot Lady in Hastings, might have an open ear to me sharing some of these local experiences. Who knows . . . maybe York will get its own pin on her official Nebraska Bigfoot Sighting map?

Bob Sautter, York News-Times, York, Nebraska, July 10, 2020, used by permission.

Bob Sautter

Bob Sautter of the York County (Nebraska) Visitors Bureau has been collecting Bigfoot stories for quite some time now. These three incidents all occurred on Nebraska Highway 81, North of York and Interstate 80.

Story Number 1

"It was dusk on a Friday night in November, 1979. I was home from college visiting my family on our farm south of Stromsburg. I headed into town to meet up with some of my high school friends who were also home. As I drove on highway 81... about 2 miles out of Burg...all of a sudden something hit the backside of my car. I quickly looked up in my rear view mirror and I'm telling you, there was a huge white hairy beast trying to hang on to the back of my vehicle. I floored it and was able to unhinge him. I turned around and headed back to the farm. I walked in, white as a ghost, and shared what had happened with my family. They did not think it was a Big Foot...but I did, and always will."

Mrs. H. A.

Story Number 2

Around 3:00 am.

"Two professional men were returning home from an out-of-town business meeting. The weather was very cold and windy. There was deep snow on the ground and it was frozen solid. They were not driving very fast because of the poor conditions. Suddenly, on the side of the road, a large, hairy creature appeared! It took only 3 steps to get across a 4-lane road! It never looked at the car or the two men inside! Instead, it kept on going, and began running across the open field. The two men looked at each other in disbelief and simultaneously said, "Did you see what I just saw??" They were stunned! They cautiously approached the spot where the creature had crossed the road, but the snow was frozen so hard they could not see any tracks on the road or in the open field! Apparently, the creature had totally disappeared from sight! Both men were absolutely terrified! They went straight home and did not return to work the next day. Neither one has spoken about the incident for many years. Mainly because of ridicule that would be forthcoming and it would be detrimental to their job security if people knew these two "crazy people" lived in their area..."

Bob Sautter

Story Number 3

The third incident also happened on Highway 81, North of York.

"It was a nice spring day and a man was driving a pickup south towards York to pick up a few groceries. Suddenly he saw a large, hairy upright animal on the side of the road! He braked quickly so he would not hit it and swerved to get in the other lane!! As he slowed down, to get past the 'THING' it grabbed a hold of the back of his pickup box and began lifting the whole truck about 3 or 4 feet up in the air and then banging it back down to the ground!! After doing this several times, the man 'gunned' the truck as hard as he could – and was able to pull away the next time the 'THING' dropped his pickup to the ground! As he sped off, the man looked in his rear view mirror and saw the "creature" standing in the middle of the road. He was shaking his fist violently and yelling and screaming in a rage!"

In my opinion, this is very unusual behavior. Some BIGFOOT may be crabby or irritable over something that happened to them recently, but to repeatedly practice the same behavior in the same area is not a common occurrence.

THESE ARE TRULY 'WEIRD' EVENTS...

Bob Sautter

Two more 'WEIRD' reports were given to me here at the MUSEUM that happened near Garrison.

Story Number 4

"On a farm nearby a family had two daughters that each had a horse. Frequently, the horses came in from the pasture to go to the stock tank for water. Both horses had their manes braided! Mom said the girls were always angry every time the horses hair was braided (because it was fairly often) and also because it was so intricately braided that it was VERY HARD to un-braid and then brush it out.

Mom said that if the daughters know BIGFOOT was suspected of being the one braiding the horses, neither one of those girls would ever ride their horses again!"

Story Number 5

"On the day before the flag mutilation, we had some hot, muggy weather. On a farm nearby, a family had some sheep. In the early afternoon, the resident lady went home to check on her sheep to make sure they weren't too warm and that they had plenty of water. All were accounted for, except for one. She could not find it... She gave up the search and left, but in the middle of the afternoon she returned and still could not find the missing lamb... In the evening, the lady continued her search for the lamb – AND – she finally found it. Its leg had been completely pulled out of the socket and the entire leg had been pulled off from the body, skin, meat, fleece and all!

The woman examined the body and could find any bite marks or deep claw marks at the wound site. (Hunters say if an animal has been attached by a bear or a mountain lion, there are definite claw indentations – BUT, there was NO EVIDENCE in this lamb's death...)"

So, WHO or WHAT pulled this animals leg out of the socket – and then ripped the hair off that enclosed the upper thigh? What kind of strength would that take???

The Killing Fields

On Sunday, August 17th 2014, I participated in an event that changed my life forever! I went on an all-lady camp-out in the heart of the Rocky Mountains!

My first day I wrote, "I have no idea what's going to happen – AND – I love it!!"

Later that evening I wrote, "I'll look back on this and smile because it was LIFE…AND I decided to LIVE IT!"

On Monday, August 18th, the rest and the best of my life began!

The day began with Robin taking us all on a walk through the meadows and the surrounding forest. As we traveled through the forest we saw many structures; arches and X's that were tightly woven together. It was just amazing! AND, it was no wind storm that had made all of these creations!

Before this, I could have seen a zillion structures, arches and X's and NEVER known that I was looking at possible BIGFOOT creations! After much teaching by example from Robin, I would easily identify these works of art.

From there, Robin took us to a place that I had NEVER heard of before, THE KILLING FIELDS, where it was believed that the BIGFOOT 'herds' deer or elk down a narrow ravine. At the end, one of his "partners" grabs the unsuspecting deer and snaps his neck or breaks one of their legs. Then, he and the family can have 'lunch.'

At the KILLING FIELD, there were bones in clumps; ribs, backbones, and jaw bones, and several different variety of animals both large and small.

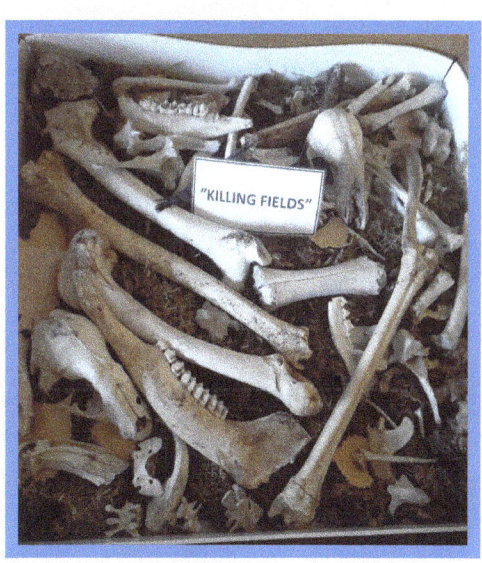

 The Killing Fields

About 10 feet from the KILLING FIELDS, there was a large boulder, about 2 feet tall and 4-5 feet in circumference. It was very beautiful there, evergreens were in the background and many colorful wild flowers surrounded this rock. I wanted to have my picture taken sitting on top, but unfortunately, I had forgotten my camera. The 'girls' promised we could return the next day and I could have my picture before we went on our hike for that day. (This was also the same location where we had seen the red eye shine the night before.)

Early the next morning, we returned to take my picture sitting on the rock. I had a REAL SURPRISE waiting for me as I walked up the hill... The first thing that I saw that was 'weird' was a smaller rock about twice the size of a bowling ball. It has been picked up and moved or thrown nearly 10 feet! Previously, it had been in the same location for quite some time. Moss had grown over the top and underneath the ground was very damp with no grass growing there. It looked like someone or something had just taken all of the grubs out...

But, my big surprise came when I got to the rock and I was preparing to sit down! At the base, on the ground was a deer's leg! And I remember distinctly that it was NOT THERE the day before! Upon closer examination, I could see that the deer's leg had been complete pulled out of the socket. There was no flesh at all left on the leg, but it had fresh blood on it that was not quite dry... It was still sticky. It was obviously a fairly fresh kill. At the joint, the leg had been twisted around at least 3 or 4 times and it was still held together by the hair and ligaments.

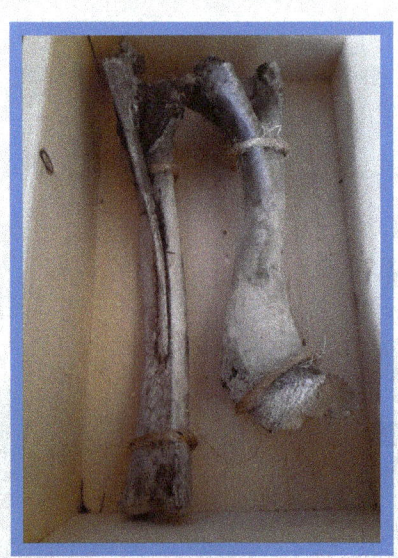

 The Killing Fields

Ligaments are a very tough, fibrous bands of connective tissue, sort of like a very tight rubber band, that holds bones together at the joints.

In order to do a feat like this, it takes an AMAZING amount of strength!!

A pathologist friend of mind, Dr. D. said it would take a minimum of 700 pounds pressure to stretch a ligament like that and then to twist it around would be nearly impossible.

Here is the whole point of this story... The lamb's leg had been pulled completely out of the hip socket (similar to the deer) and then was pulled completely out of its body. The flesh, meat and wool were completely torn away, leaving the leg totally detached. So, who or what did this???

THE MISSING LEG HAS NEVER BEEN FOUND...

The Killing Fields

"That plats the manes of horses in the night;
and bakes the elflocks in foul, sluttish hairs,
Which once untangled, much misfortune bodes..."

William Shakespeare

The definition of this word, 'elflocks' is a "tangled lock of hair, in unusual disorder as if done by the elves..."

Little was written by the Celts, Britons and Druids, so it's hard to pinpoint the exact moment in time that the word elflocks emerged, but archaeological finds like Stonehenge can attest that these cultures may be traced back as far as 2000 B.C. and beyond.

You see, even in Shakespeare's time and beyond, the mystery of the BRAIDED HORSES was a puzzlement. Evidently, these questions are nothing new...even to this day...

AND...

In China, the first people to begin braiding the horse's hair lived in about the 15th Century. The braiding was done in various clans – that was somewhat equivalent to branding cattle.

...Nevertheless, what is here, down for the record may prove to be the only true important and very first stepping stone into all future plaiting discoveries that will completely jam wide open the long locked doors of Pandora's mysterious Box?

Don Monroe

We all have our opinions and what we believe is substantial evidence to support them. So, NOW I will submit this for your approval and analysis; inviting you to draw your own individual conclusion as to what may have occurred that 'WEIRD' fateful MEMORIAL DAY WEEKEND in the CEMETERY.......

in Garrison, Nebraska.

Flag Retirement Ceremony

Veteran's Day, November 11, 2020

This ceremony was held in David City, Nebraska, in Butler County. Garrison is only a few miles away and is also in Butler County.

(The Garrison flag was originally taken to the Butler County Sheriff for inspection. Later, it was also scheduled to be burned at the Retirement Ceremony, but was "saved" due to very strong wind. Later, the Garrison Cemetery Board decided to donate to the desecrated flag to the BIGFOOT MUSEUM. We believe this to be an important part of American History and needed to be investigated further...)

On Veteran's Day, flags were flying on the Courthouse Lawn. Members of the various Military Branches were present as well as members of the American Legion and the Veterans of Foreign Wars.

Flag Retirement Ceremony

A short, memorial program was held, as well as a rifle salute.

 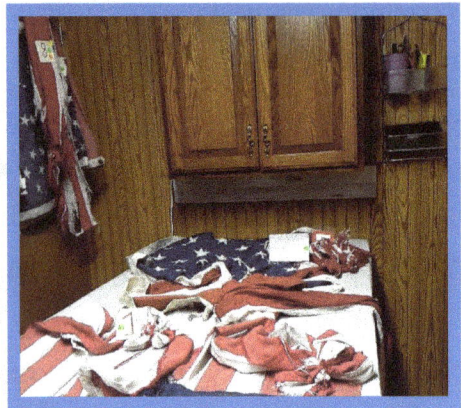

Following the rifle salute, taps was played by Larry Sabata (in the white helmet) and the remembrance portion of the ceremony was officially over.

From there, at the Retirement Ceremony, veterans respectfully unfolded many flags and proceeded to burn them. As the flags were being prepared to be burned, they were all carefully inspected by the veterans in attendance. If they had been braided or knotted, they were given to us for further inspection and investigation. Out of these flags, 13 were found to be torn and either knotted, braided, or both. At the end of the Retirement Ceremony, we were given these 13 flags for the Museum. We promised to honor and respect these flags just like the veterans in attendance were doing.

13 Flags

13 Flags, 13 Stripes, 13 Colonies

Disclaimer:

The 13 flags were donated to the Nebraska Bigfoot Museum after the Retirement Ceremony. As the information behind the remaining twelve flags are unknown, we do not know the exact date the flags were torn and braided; therefore, the weather conditions or any possibly related occurrences are unknown.

 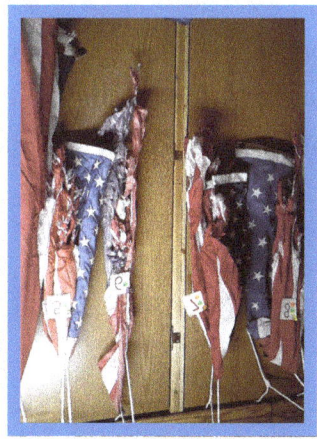 

13 Flags

Flag #1 was given to the American Legion on November 10, 2020, the very day before the flag retirement ceremony in Butler County. This flag was torn and braided between November 8th and 9th 2020. The flag came from a farm that was about 3-4 miles from Garrison, and for many years the farmer that lives there had always had a flag flying in his yard. In all those years, not one flag had ever been damaged until that fateful night. On eighth of November, an ice storm traveled through the area.

Upon research and investigation, Tamara, our Research Analyst, discovered that on Sunday, November 8th, 2020, the area was windy with gusts up to 35-40 miles per hour. The wind continued into Monday and Tuesday, on November 9th and 10th; however, ranged between 20-30 miles per hour in conjunction with an ice storm during this period with rain, snow, mist, and freezing fog. Even though we had all of these multiple weather factors, we haven't found a flag that was torn and braided due to wind.

13 Flags

Flag # 3

Flag # 3 has
2 long braids
1 braid is approximately
20 inches long

1 braid is approximately
12 inches long.

Both have very hard, tight knots about every 2 inches

Flag # 13

Has 2 braids
similiar

Both are braided
with a hard knot
at the end

1st. braid about 7
    inches long

2nd braid about
4 inches long.

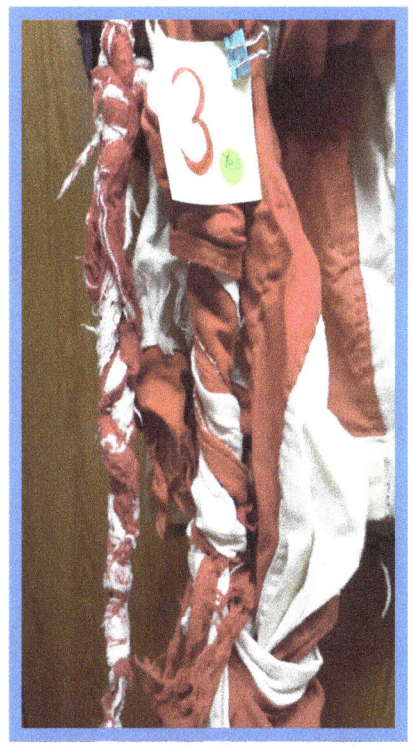

Details of flags #3 and #13

13 Flags

Four more braided and knotted flags.

Flag #8

13 Flags

 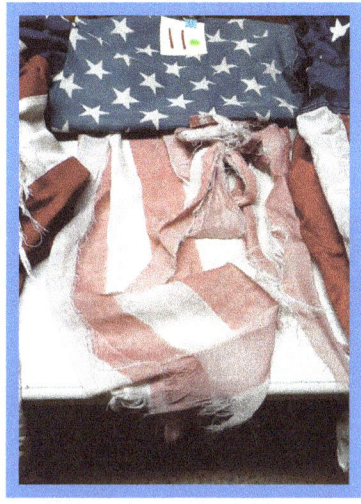 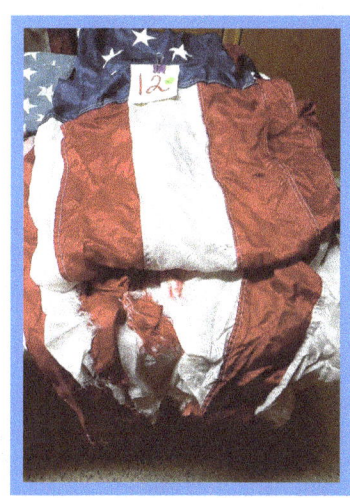

Flags #10 through #12

Flag #13

Don Monroe - U.S. Navy

Don Monroe is a Navy veteran and this is a report and story of a few Navy ships he served aboard.

U.S.S Falgout[1]

The U.S.S. Falgout was Don's first ship. Out of 365 days in a year he was on a total of 324 days a year for 28 months. This was a weather ship in the Pacific Ocean off the Alaskan Coast and Russia. They went as far North as the ice packs. The Falgout's home port was Seattle, Washington, Pier 91.

Don Monroe while serving on the U.S.S. Falgout

---

1   The U.S. Navy radar picket destroyer escort USS Falgout (DER-324) underway at sea off Pearl Harbor, Hawaii, on 30 August 1963. US Navy photo from Navsource.org

 Don Monroe – U.S. Navy

The sailors were on board each voyage for approximately 28-40 days depending on their destination.

During these voyages, there were many very severe wild storm watches. The ship had to go right into 'the eye of the storm' and then sent weather reports back to the mainland.

The U.S.S. Falgout was the first naval ship to ever have an African American Commander, Lt. Commander Samuel L. Gravely made Naval history in 1962. The Navy said he was the first African American to command a U.S. Warship. He later rose to the rank of Vice Admiral, also a first among African American navymen.

Vice Admiral Samuel L. Gravely

Don Monroe - U.S. Navy

U.S.S. Forrestal

The U.S.S Forrestal was based in Seattle, Washington and Hawaii.

U.S.S. General W. A. Mann

Photos US Navy from Navsource.com

Don Monroe - U.S. Navy

U.S.S. Wilhoite

U.S.S. Staten Island

Photos US Navy from Navsource.com

 Don Monroe - U.S. Navy

U.S.S. Vance

Don was on was on all of these ships. They were the WILDEST, ROUGHEST, MOST DANGEROUS ships to be on for sea duty that was possible during the 1950s.

These ships were from 306 up to 1067 feet long and the width (beam) was 36 up to 238 feet.

These ships were considered to be like 'floating jails' because once you were on board, you couldn't get off...

These ships were very SONAR and RADAR heavy. Often waves completely encircled the ships. The waves were 15-20 feet high. These ships averaged over 300 days per year at sea.

Photo US Navy from Navsource.com

 Don Monroe - U.S. Navy

Sometimes the FLAGS were frayed due to VERY STRONG WINDS and constant water spraying on them.

The sailing flags were always 'UP.' They showed the various countries and they could be seen from a long distance. If the FLAGS were 'frayed', they were trimmed a little.

The Navy changed FLAGS immediately whenever they had a chance.

HOWEVER,

"The Flags I saw were NEVER BRAIDED!

Even in the EYE OF THE STORM!"

Don Monroe said, "75% of the world is water, but I never saw one torn or braided flag, so it must be a land animal doing this."[1]

---

1 Don Monroe says "it is good to compare comparables": You can see video showing a flag flown on a platform 34 miles off the coast and tattered by the winds of hurricane Florence, in which it appears to get torn up and knotted, at https://www.youtube.com/ TTwatch?v=5S7Bz4nl1js At about 1:50 in this video the lowest stripe begins tearing and by 2:15 the lowest three stripes have split all the way to the header. One picture of the end result is found at https://twitter.com/Local12Tessa/status/1047892480417517578/photo/2. A related picture is at https://apnews.com/article/00c6b904d8e940459a338a25d3928346. Additional tattered flags are on display at the Frying Pan Shoals Tower https://www.starnewsonline.com/story/news/local/2020/09/17/battle-save-frying-pan-tower-underway-32-miles-offshore/5822278002/ at about 5:24. All accessed March 29, 2021.

Bruce - U.S. Navy

A lifelong friend of mine, who wishes to remain anonymous, is a Navy veteran and a retired police offer. My friend, let's call him Bruce, served in the Navy for over 4 years. Bruce went on to serve as a police officer in Omaha, Nebraska, for over 20 years with the majority of the time in a squad car.

Bruce stated that during his time in the Navy he served on three different ships. Each of these ships, as all Navy ships, flew the required Colors or flags no matter the weather or sea conditions. According to Bruce, the flags would become frayed and torn in rough seas, high winds or severe storms. The flags were changed as soon as possible depending on the weather conditions and mission requirements. Bruce stated that he never saw a braided flag during his service or heard of a braided flag on a ship.

Bruce stated that during his time as a police officer, he would notice U.S. flags flown at banks, stores, gas stations, personal homes, etc. Bruce stated that he noticed flags that were ripped, torn, faded and sometimes twisted for flags that had been outside for a long period of time; however, he never witnessed a braided flag,

Bruce also has a U.S. flag at his house which he has flown since his time in the Navy. Bruce stated he has his flag flown 24/7 with a light shining on it at night at 25 feet in the air. He usually changes his flag about every 4-6 months as the flag will begin to fray and fade after about this period of time. Bruce stated that he has never seen his flags torn and ripped overnight. Bruce also stated that he has never had any of his flags braided after a storm or otherwise.

When I discussed the incident of the Garrison flag with Bruce, he did not know how this could have occurred overnight due to a storm. He stated that if Bigfoot had done this task, maybe it was something they had learned from the Native Americans prior to the U.S. settlement.

Tamara Stier

Tamara Stier

Research Analyst

MUFON Field Investigator

Joe – U.S. Air Force

I also have a friend, who wishes to be anonymous, that I have known for over fifteen years who served in the U.S. Air Force and was a Boy Scout Master. My friend, let's call him Joe, served in the U.S. Air Force for over 17 years. Joe has also been involved in the Boy Scouts for over 30 years and has been a Scout Master for over 10 years.

When Joe was in the Air Force he was a member of the Honors Guard Colors Flight during the majority of his time in the military. Joe stated that as part of the Honors Guard, the Flags would be raised in the morning and taken down at night. In addition, the Flags were normally taken down during a storm. Joe stated that during his time in the Air Force, he had never seen or heard of a braided flag.

After Joe's service in the Air Force, he became active in the Boy Scouts with his sons. He has been involved in the Boy Scouts for over 30 years and has been a Scout Master for over 10 years.

Joe - U.S. Air Force

 He stated that as part of the Boy Scouts, flag retirement ceremonies are performed on a regular basis. Joe has a saying, "Boy Scouts is where old flags go to die." Joe stated that during almost every camp outing, which happens a few times each year, they do a flag retirement ceremony as they receive quite a few flags for retirement. Joe stated he and the other scout leaders have to keep a close eye on the scouts as most 10-year-old boys are a little too fascinated with fires sometimes. Joe stated that they would inspect the flags prior to retirement and he has noticed flags that were torn, ripped, faded, some that were twisted, and some that had a few small knots; however, he has never seen a braided flag in his 30 years in the scouts. Joe stated that the flags the Boy Scout troops he worked with received flags from the Omaha, Nebraska area. Joe wasn't sure how many flags he had retired; however, he guesstimated that he has been part of 100-150 flag retirement ceremonies.

 Joe stated he has his flag flown 24/7 with a light shining on it at night since he left the military. Joe stated that he has never seen his flags torn and ripped overnight. Joe also stated that he has never had any of his flags braided after a storm or otherwise.

Tamara Stier

Tamara Stier

Research Analyst

MUFON Field Investigator

 # Little Sioux Baskets

 Little Sioux Baskets

These baskets were donated to the museum by Mr. Don Monroe. The story is true and it possibly began 30 or 40 years ago.

Don and his wife, Marion, crisscrossed our country many times; exploring, hiking and camping. In between their adventures, they attended sport shows, trade shows and visited antique stores and flea markets. They met many VERY INTERESTING PEOPLE along the way... One of them was a Native American woman named Betty Blackbear. She was a Sioux. Don has tried to find her again, but to date he has had no luck... So, I will tell her story as I have heard it...

Betty, for many years made various Indian trinkets and gifts that she could sell or trade with passing travelers. Don and Marion became two of her customers. They obtained a 'one of a kind' gift!! Betty had 3 miniature baskets...they were so small; only about $\frac{1}{4}$ inch in diameter! And, the AMAZING THING IS, they were braided or woven probably using sweet grass. Just gazing at them, it looks like an IMPOSSIBLE FEAT!

This is where the story ends...in the course of their travels, they lost track of Betty, but they NEVER lost the LITTLE SIOUX BASKETS. Recently, Don donated the BASKETS to the BIGFOOT MUSEUM. Since then, I have thought about these three BASKETS a great deal... I want to know their HISTORY, and I want to know WHERE THEY CAME FROM!! But, most of all, I want to know, who was taught to weave or braid the grass or straw like that? Was it Betty? Or her Mother? Or possibly old Grandmother? Or possibly some other woman in her tribe? Was this a Sioux tradition of the Blackbears? Was this skill passed down through many generations? And what about Betty? Or some other young girl)? Or a teenager? Did they have small nimble fingers? Did they learn this skill as a child; and then NEVER forgot it? (It is said that the Blackfeet tribe of Montana also make little baskets, but theirs are made out of pine needles.)

 Little Sioux Baskets

So, what does all of this have to do with BRAIDED FLAGS? I took a closer look at some of the horses' manes that are braided and are on display in the MUSEUM. Some of them are VERY SMALL...and VERY INTRICATE... And then, I looked again at some of the braids on the flag from Garrison... AND, some of them are also VERY SMALL and INTRICATE... AND THEN, I looked at the LITTLE BASKETS again...they are also VERY SMALL and INTRICATE... and I really believe, if you learn a skill as a child, and practice that skill often, you will NEVER FORGET IT!!

Often, guests to the Museum ask me, "how a BIGFOOT COULD EVER HAVE BRAIDED A HORSES MANE, because their hands are so big??" And I wonder, could one of their kids have possibly made the extra small horse braids? OR did one of their kids make the SUPER SMALL BRAIDS on the FLAG?? (Some are only one inch long, made with only 2 strands...) AND, did one of their kids make the miniature BASKETS? So, please study these photographs and make up your own mind...

 Garrison, NE, Flag – 2020

'Something', May 24, 2020, tore flag into small strips and braided them.[1]

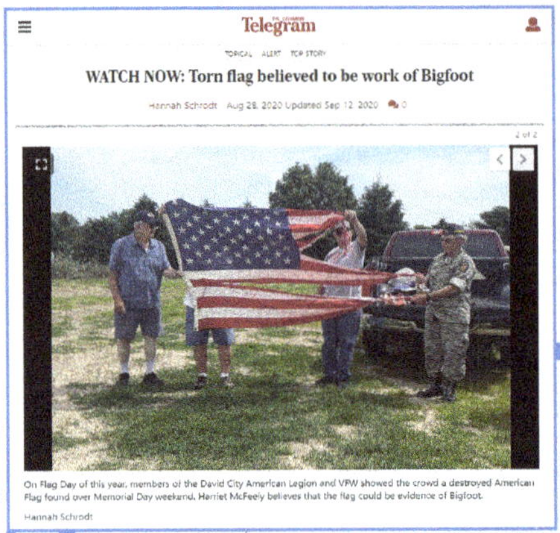

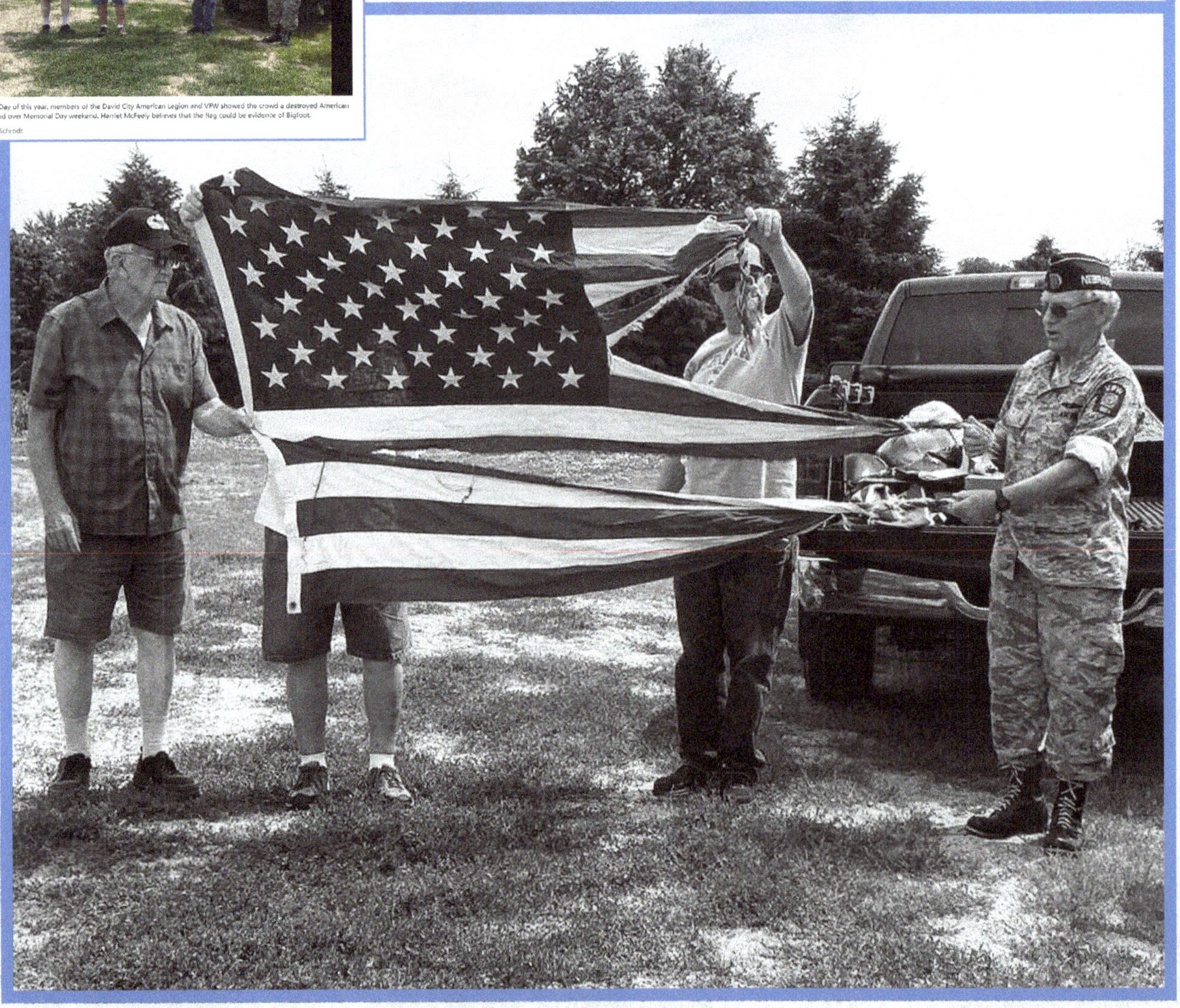

1   Photo: Hannah Schrodt, The Banner-Press, David City, Nebraska June 18, 2020. The detail image above has been altered from the original: Specifically, it has been rendered in greyscale and cropped for comparison to the 1917 image on the opposite page.

 Washington, DC, Flag - 1917

'Wind Storm', Jan. 16, 1917, tore flag into small strips and braided them[1]

---

1   Harris & Ewing, photographer. (1917) Wind Storm, Tore Flag Into Small Strips and Braided Them. United States, 1917. [Photograph] Retrieved from the Library of Congress, https://www.loc.gov/item/2016887072/

Inset: Flag above the House Wing of the U.S. Capitol (right). Theodor Horydczak Collection (ca. 1920 to ca. 1950), Library of Congress, Prints and Photographs Division. https://hdl.loc.gov/loc.pnp/thc.5a37556. This image has been cropped from the original and adjusted for contrast.

Washington, DC, Flag – 1917

It was a brisk winter morning on Tuesday, January 16, 1917 in Washington, D.C. The temperature high for the day was 28°F and the low temperature was 20°F. It was 2½ years since the start of the Great War (World War I) and the United States remained neutral. Woodrow Wilson was the President of the United States and had been re-elected with the slogan "He Kept Us Out of The War."

The House of Representatives met at 11:00 am at the Capital Building and considered various bills including an immigration bill, post office appropriation bill which restored pneumatic tube service, a revenue bill, and a public buildings appropriation bill.

The previous night on January 15, 1917, the Annual Charity Ball for the Children's Hospital was held and for the first time, the President and the First Lady attended this gala. Prior to the charity ball, the President entertained distinguished guests at the White House including the German ambassador. The President and Mrs. Wilson arrived at the charity ball at about 11:00 pm and remained until after midnight. In addition, government and military officials along with prominent members of society entertained guests with several attending the charity ball after hosting their dinners.

The major event which occurred on this same day on January 16, 1917, was the 'Zimmermann Telegram' which was sent by German Foreign Secretary Arthur Zimmermann. This telegram was a coded secret letter sent to Heinrich von Eckardt, the German ambassador to Mexico via normal diplomatic correspondence allowed by the neutral United States. The secret letter stated:

> "On the 1st of February we intend to begin submarine warfare unrestricted. In spite of this, it is our intention to endeavor to keep neutral the United States of America. If this attempt is not successful, we propose an alliance on the following basis with Mexico: That we shall make war together and together make peace. We shall give general financial support, and it is understood that Mexico is to reconquer the lost territory in New Mexico, Texas and Arizona. The details are left to you for settlement."

The German ambassador was also instructed to utilize the Mexican president to assist in persuading Japan to join the Central Powers.

British Intelligence intercepted this telegram and deciphered the secret message. Once the secret message was disclosed to the U.S. and made public, it was the final major factor for the entry of the U.S. into World War I.

Washington, DC, Flag - 1917

During my research into possible additional braided flags, I came across two pictures from 1917 which had 'braided flag' in the titles. The pictures of the flag in this chapter are located in the Library of Congress. The flag pictured was located on the National Capital Building in Washington, D.C. over the House of Representatives. Two pictures of this flag were taken on January 16, 1917 and donated to the Library of Congress in 1955 by photography studio Harris & Ewing, Inc. This photography studio was started in 1905 in Washington, D.C. by George W. Harris and Martha Ewing. This studio became very prestigious and one of primary photography studios for government officials including Presidents in Washington, D.C.

When George W. Harris retired, he donated 70,000 glass and film negatives to the Library Congress. The two pictures do not have a corresponding news story; however, both have detailed titles. The first picture is entitled, "Flag flying above House of Rep. tore into strips and braided perfectly by wind storm, Jan 16, 1917". The second picture is entitled, "Wind storm, Jan. 16, 1917, tore flag into small strips and braided them." The gentlemen in the pictures are not identified; however, based upon pictures of George W. Harris[1] and the fact that he was the primary photographer until 1955, the gentlemen on the right of each of these pictures appears to be Mr. Harris. I reviewed local newspapers on the date and surrounding dates of Jan. 16th 1917 for weather reports and local news stories.

George W. Harris

---

1   Harris & Ewing, photographer. H & E photographer. , None. [Between 1910 and 1920] [Photograph] Retrieved from the Library of Congress, https://www.loc.gov/item/2016854657/.

 Washington, DC, Flag – 1917

Flag flying above House of Rep. tore into strips and braided perfectly by wind storm, Jan 16, 1917[1]

1. Harris & Ewing, photographer. (1917) Flag flying above House of Rep. tore into strips and braided perfectly by wind storm. United States Washington D.C. District of Columbia Washington D.C, 1917. [Photograph] Retrieved from the Library of Congress, https://www.loc.gov/item/2016887073/.

 Washington, DC, Flag - 1917

Details from the 1917 braided flag pictures.

 Weather Reports - 1917

The Evening Star - Jan. 15, 1917
Washington, D.C.

The Evening Star - Jan. 16, 1917
Washington, D.C.

According to the Washington D.C. Evening Star (evening) newspaper that the weather on January 15, 1917 predicted snow overnight with a low of 20 with fresh northeast and east winds.[1] On January 16, 1917 the records for the preceding 24 hours included a low of 20°F and an afternoon high of 27°F, predicting fair overnight with moderate northerly winds.[2] And reporting on January 17th the overnight low had been 17°F, rising to 39°F by afternoon. Similar values were reported in the Washington Herald, the morning paper. The term 'fresh breeze' translates to a moderate wind, 19 to 24 mph, enough to sway large branches and small trees and form crested waves on lakes. The term 'fresh gale' was also in use, for winds 39-46 mph, but the weather report would certainly have mentioned a gale. In these weather reports no mention of abnormal or otherwise remarkable wind events was found.

---

1   Evening Star. (Washington, DC) 15 Jan. 1917. Retrieved from the Library of Congress, www.loc.gov/item/sn83045462/1917-01-15/ed-1/
2   Evening Star. (Washington, DC) 16 Jan. 1917, p. 1. Retrieved from the Library of Congress, www.loc.gov/item/sn83045462/1917-01-16/ed-1/

Weather Reports – 1917

WEATHER.

Fair tonight and tomorrow; continued cold; lowest temperature tonight about 16 degrees; northerly winds.
Temperature for twenty-four hours ending 2 p.m.: Highest, 27, at 2 p.m. today; lowest, 20, at 8 p.m. yesterday.
Full report on page 10.

WEATHER.

For the District of Columbia, partly overcast tonight and tomorrow; rising temperature; lowest temperature tonight about 25 degrees; fresh southwest winds.

For Virginia, partly overcast tonight and tomorrow; warmer in north and southeast portions tonight; moderate to fresh southwest winds.

For Maryland, partly overcast tonight and tomorrow; warmer tonight; fresh southwest winds.

For West Virginia, overcast and warmer tonight. Tomorrow unsettled, probably local snows.

Tide Tables.

(Compiled by United States coast and geodetic survey.)
Today—Low tide, 8:29 a.m. and 9:35 p.m.; high tide, 1:52 a.m. and 2:26 p.m.
Tomorrow—Low tide, 9:26 a.m. and 10:36 p.m.; high tide, 2:49 a.m. and 3:24 p.m.

The Sun and Moon.

Today—Sun rose, 7:25 a.m.; sun sets, 5:13 p.m.
Tomorrow—Sun rises, 7:24 a.m.; sun sets, 5:13 p.m.
Moon rises, 1:34 a.m.; sets, 11:42 a.m.
Automobiles lamps to be lighted one-half hour after sunset.

Records for Twenty-Four Hours.

The following were the readings of the thermometer and barometer at the weather bureau for the twenty-four hours beginning at 2 p.m. yesterday:
Thermometer—Yesterday, 4 p.m., 28; 8 p.m., 26; 12 midnight, 23; today, 4 a.m., 22; 8 a.m., 20; 12 noon, 34; 2 p.m., 39. Maximum, 39, at 2 p.m. today; minimum, 17, at 7 a.m. today.

Also, based upon the news stories per the Washington Herald Newspaper and Washington D.C.–The Evening Star Newspaper on January 16, 1917[1,2], no significant weather or wind was reported and no changes to normal and scheduled events occurred due to weather issues. The Washington D.C. Herald Newspapers from Jan. 9, 1917 through Jan. 14, 1917 were also reviewed and no significant weather issues and no severe or gale force winds were reported, except for strong northwest winds noted on Jan. 10.

1 Evening Star. (Washington, DC) 16 Jan. 1917, p. 1. Retrieved from the Library of Congress, www.loc.gov/item/sn83045462/1917-01-16/ed-1/
2 Evening Star. (Washington, DC) 17 Jan. 1917, p. 10, https://www.loc.gov/resource/sn83045462/1917-01-17/ed-1/?sp=10

 Weather Reports - 1917

The Washington, D.C. weather reports noted in the local newspapers do not mention a storm or high winds on Jan. 15, 1917 or Jan. 16, 1917. While it's possible the flag had been in a storm sometime before this picture, the weather reports for the week prior to do not list a storm or high winds.

In addition, the titles of both pictures imply that this occurred on Jan. 16, 1917. Per current procedures, the U.S. Flag is flown over the House of Representatives while they are in session and according to Washington, D.C. newspaper, The Evening Star, the House of Representatives was in session starting at 11:00 am on Jan. 16, 1917. It is also possible that the flag was flown longer than when the House was in session; however, the picture description states that the damage to the flag and the braiding occurred in a short period of time after a wind storm. I am unsure of the meaning of this; however, the similarity between this incident and the Garrison flag incident is very intriguing.

Tamara Stier

Tamara Stier
Research Analyst
MUFON Field Investigator

 Weather Reports - 2020

The weather records were reviewed for the Garrison area for the days of the Garrison flag incident on May 23, 2020 and May 24, 2020. Two weather websites which maintain historical weather data were reviewed: weatherunderground.com and weatherspark.com. The Weather Underground website is utilized for MUFON (Mutual UFO Network) to document the weather conditions at the time of MUFON cases. The weather data available at Weather Underground for the days in review was limited to the Lincoln Airport in Lincoln, NE airport (LNK) weather data. This airport is approximately 50 miles southeast of Garrison, NE. Weather Spark had weather data available from the Columbus Municipal Airport in Columbus, NE (KOLU). This airport is approximately 30 miles northeast of Garrison, NE.

On May 23, 2020

The high temperature for the day was 79°F and the low temperature was 59°F. The maximum wind speed for this day was 15 mph and the weather was cloudy to partly cloudy. This weather was the same on both weather websites.

On May 24, 2020

The high temperature for the day was 77°F and the low temperature was 60°F. A thunderstorm went through Garrison at about 3:00 am. According to the Columbus Airport, this thunderstorm occurred from approximately 3:00 am until 05:00 am. During this thunderstorm, the wind speed ranged from 18.3 mph to 31.1 mph with gusts ranging from 24.2 mph to 38.0 mph. According to this historical radar data from NOAA (National Oceanic and Atmospheric Administration), this thunderstorm gained strength from Columbus, NE through Lincoln, NE. According to the Lincoln Airport, this thunderstorm occurred approximately from 3:00 am to 5:00 am. During this thunderstorm, the wind speed ranged from 20 mph to 35 mph with gusts ranging from 24 mph to 51 mph.

I believe it is safe to assume that the wind speed and gusts during this thunderstorm was probably somewhere in between the data collected at Columbus and Lincoln. While this storm did go through Garrison at the time of the flag incident, strong winds and storms are common in Nebraska.

Weather Reports - 2020

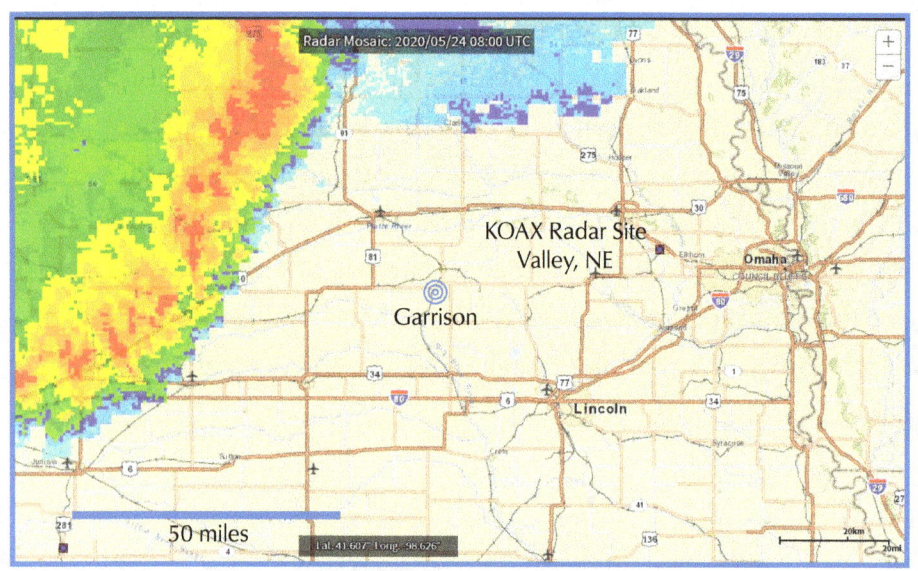

Weather radar reflectivity mosaic,[1] May 24, 2020, 08:00 UTC, 03:00 CDT.

A fast moving weather front brought rain to the Garrison area early on the morning of May 24, 2020, averaging 0.64" among 20 rain gauges in Butler and nearby counties.

May 24, 2020, 09:00 UTC, 04:00 CDT.

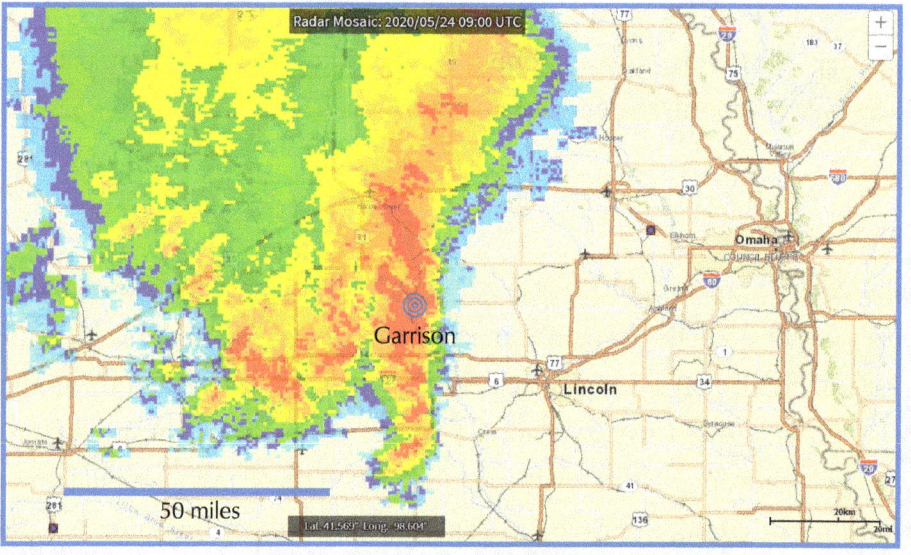

May 24, 2020, 09:00 UTC, 05:00 CDT.

1 https://gis.ncdc.noaa.gov/maps/ncei/radar

Weather Reports - 2020

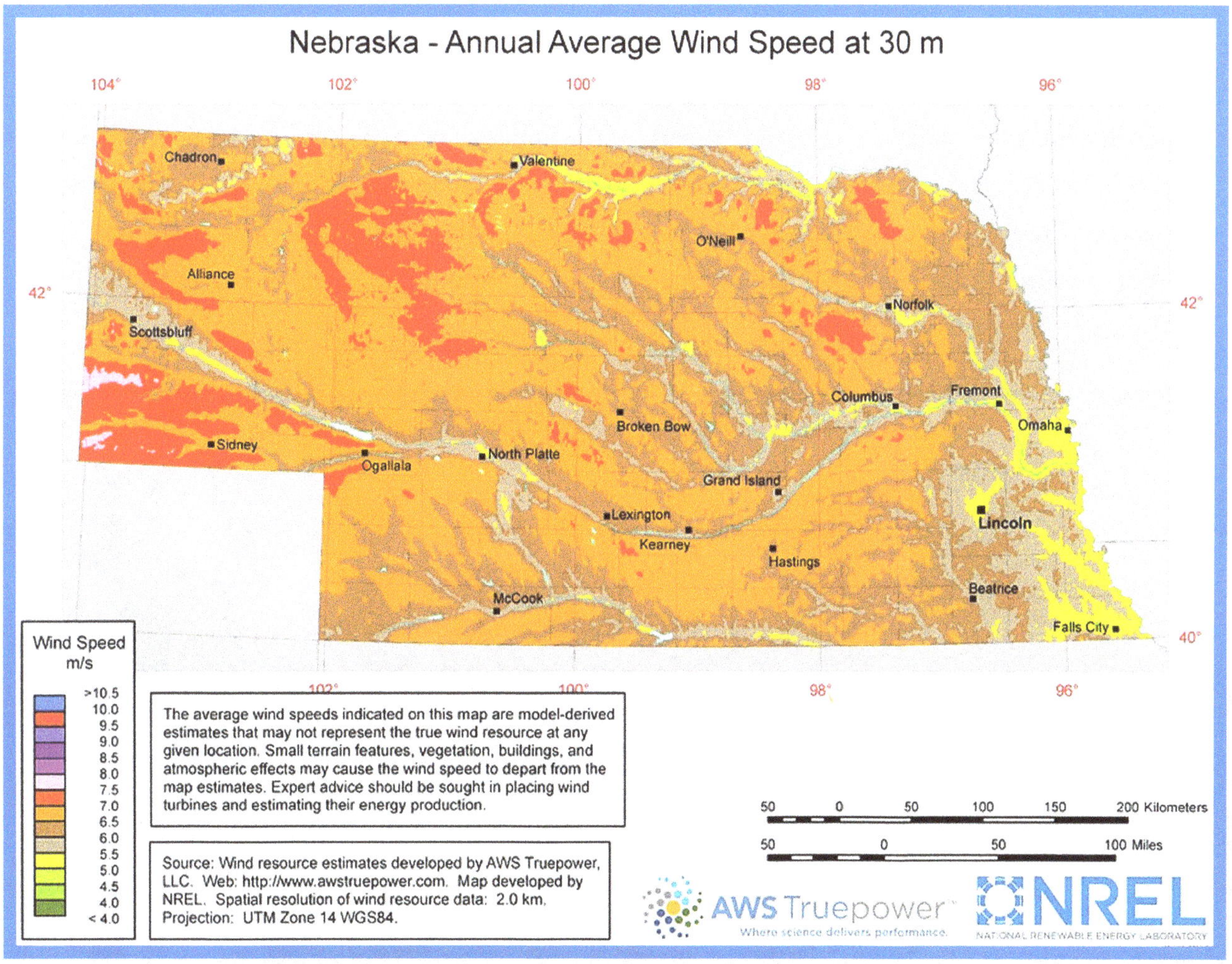

Nebraska Wind Map

Weather Reports - 2020

According to the Nebraska Wind Energy and Wildlife Project and the U.S. Department of Energy, Nebraska is ranked fourth in the U.S. for potential wind power generation. The maps (on this and the previous page) from the U.S. Department of Energy show the Annual Average of Wind Speed.

As you can see from these maps, the majority of Nebraska and the Midwest have average wind speeds in the 8.0-8.5 m/s (~17.9 – 19.0 mph) at 80 meters (262 feet) and 7.0-7.5 m/s (~15.7 – 16.78 mph) at 30 meters (98 feet).

NOAA also has a report for average wind speeds and average maximum wind gusts per month from 1930-1996 as shown in the chart on the previous page. In Grand Island, NE which is about 70 miles southwest of Garrison, NE, the average mean wind speed ranged from 10 – 14 mph and the average peak gust ranged from 49 – 80 mph. In Lincoln, NE which is about 50 miles southeast of Garrison, NE, the average mean wind speed ranged from 8 – 12 mph and the average peak gust ranged from 40 – 83 mph.

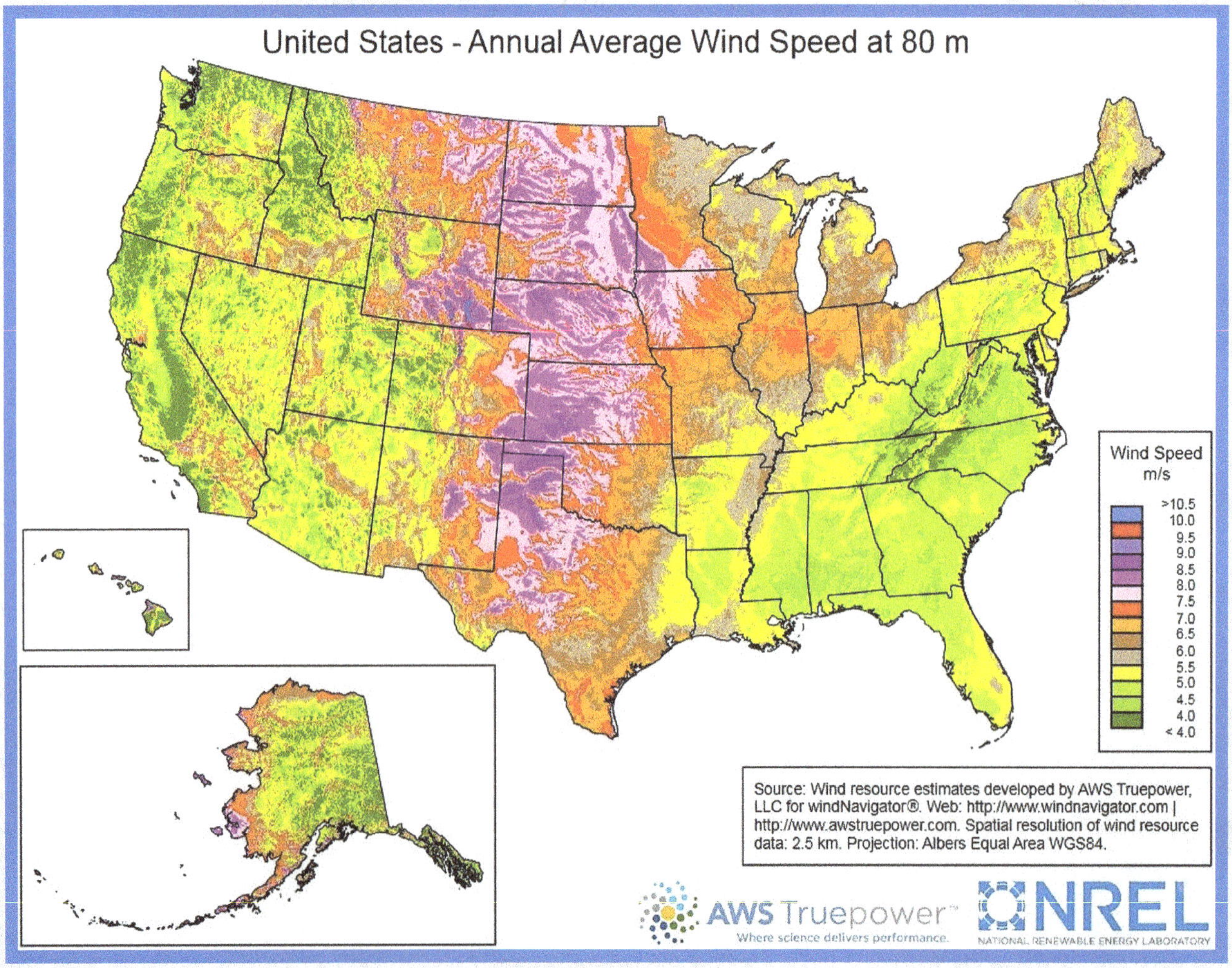

Weather Reports - 2020

NATIONAL CLIMATIC DATA CENTER
151 PATTON AVENUE ROOM 120
ASHEVILLE, NC 28801-5001
(NCDC)

PHONE : (828) 271-4800   INTERNET : orders@ncdc.noaa.gov
FACSIMILE : (828) 271-4876   WEB site : http://www.ncdc.noaa.gov

November 1998

CLIMATIC WIND DATA FOR THE UNITED STATES

The climatic wind data contained in this summary was extracted from the NCDC's Local Climatological Data publication, Navy & Air Force climatic briefs, and other sources. Locations are not all inclusive and wind data may be available for sites not listed in this summary. The total period of this summary is 1930-1996. The period of record (POR) for which wind data is summarized varies for individual sites and may begin and end at any time during the 1930-1996 period. All available wind data is provided regardless of POR or source. Updated data for many sites can be obtained from post 1996 Local Climatological Data annual publications.

In the table, prevailing wind directions (DIR) are given in compass points; mean wind speeds (SPD) and peak gust (PGU) are in miles per hour (mph). When peak gust (PGU) wind velocities are not available, fastest-mile or 5-second winds may be substituted. This will be indicated by a $ for fastest-mile and # for 5-second winds preceding PGU (ie: $PGU = fastest-mile winds). Wind types may be combined to reflect the highest reported wind. When appropriate wind data is not available, an N/A will appear in lieu of data.

Conversion tables of miles per hour to knots and compass points to degrees are provided at the end of this wind table.

****

		JAN	FEB	MAR	APR	MAY	JUN	JUL	AUG	SEP	OCT	NOV	DEC	ANN
NEBRASKA														
Grand Island	DIR	N	N	N	N	N	N	N	N	S	S	S	S	S
	SPD	12	12	13	14	13	12	11	10	11	11	12	12	12
	#PGU	64	59	61	60	80	77	72	66	46	61	51	49	80
Lincoln	DIR	N	N	N	N	N	N	N	N	N	N	N	N	N
	SPD	9	9	11	12	10	9	9	8	9	9	9	9	9
	#PGU	53	52	52	47	83	56	71	53	56	57	40	49	83
Norfolk	DIR	NNW	NNW	NNW	NNW	S	S	S	S	S	NNW	NNW	NW	S
	SPD	12	12	14	14	12	11	10	10	11	11	12	12	12
	PGU	60	56	63	66	54	59	78	82	71	56	55	60	82
N. Platte	DIR	WNW	WNW	NW	NW	N	N	N	N	SSE	SSE	S	S	NW
	SPD	9	10	12	13	12	10	10	9	10	10	10	9	10
	PGU	64	55	64	76	72	64	68	74	58	68	60	56	76
Omaha(Eppley)	DIR	NNW	NNW	N	N	NNW	NNW	SSE	SSE	S	S	S	S	SSE
	SPD	11	11	12	13	11	10	9	9	9	10	11	11	11
	$PGU	57	57	73	65	73	72	109	66	47	62	56	52	109
ScottsBluff	DIR	WNW	WNW	WNW	WNW	WNW	WNW	WNW	WNW	WNW	WNW	ESE	ESE	WNW
	SPD	11	11	13	13	12	11	9	9	9	10	11	11	11
	PGU	68	62	59	63	63	70	68	66	54	60	61	66	70
Valentine	DIR	NW	NNW	NNW	NNW	S	SSE	SSE	S	S	WNW	WNW	WNW	NW
	SPD	9	9	10	10	10	10	9	8	10	9	9	9	9
	#PGU	53	63	52	60	41	45	39	60	51	55	37	51	63

Weather Reports - 2020

In addition, tornadoes occur each spring and early summer in Nebraska. According to NOAA, the average annual tornadoes in Nebraska is approximately 57 per year as per the map below.

Thee map opposite, also from NOAA, shows the location of tornadoes in the U.S. in 2011 with 55 tornadoes occurring in Nebraska.

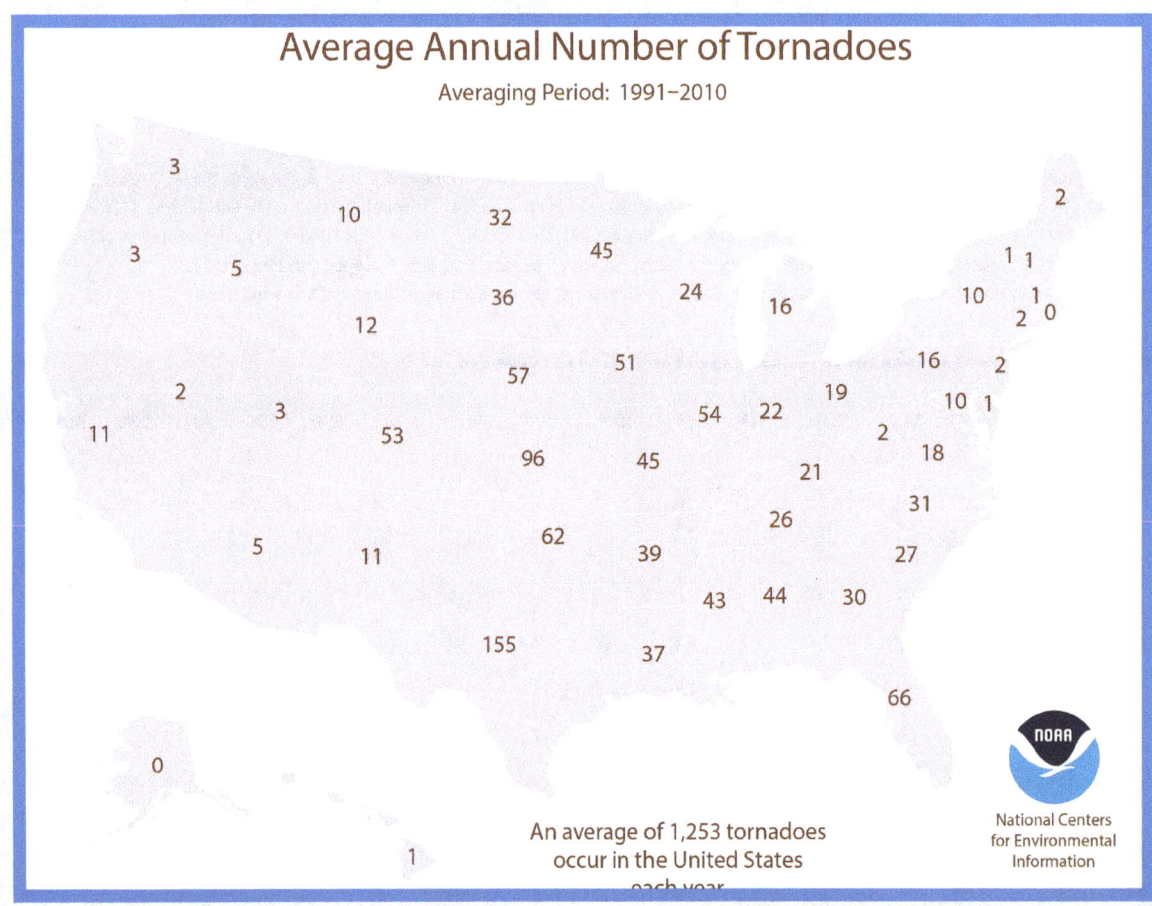

Weather Reports - 2020

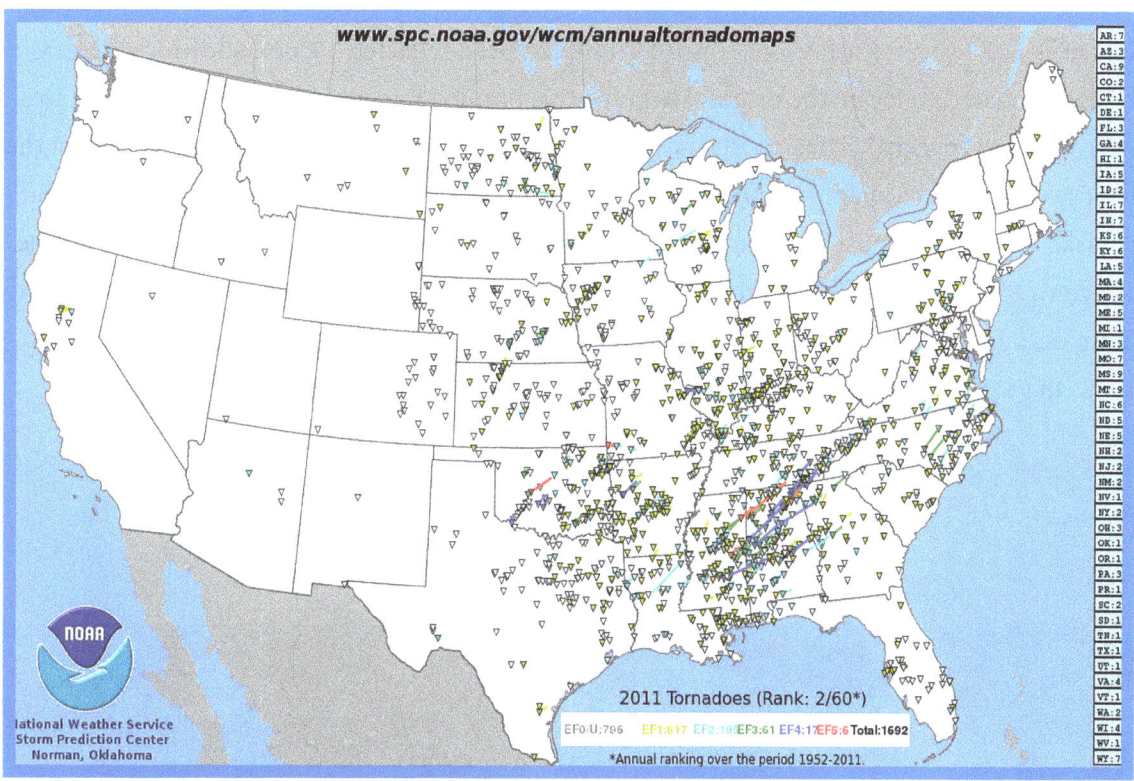

    After reviewing the weather data on May 23rd and 24th in 2020 along with the review of the historical and average weather and wind patterns in Nebraska, if the wind and/or thunderstorms caused the Garrison flag to be torn and braided during the two-hour thunderstorm which was an average to moderately above average thunderstorm in Nebraska, wouldn't there be many torn and braided flags and windsocks on a regular basis?

Tamara Stier

Tamara Stier

Research Analyst

MUFON Field Investigator

 Grand Island, Nebraska

During the research into braided flags, an image came up as a result of this search on Reddit and Imgur with a U.S. flag with one large braid. The information regarding this flag was on a social media; however, the personal information had been redacted. Upon additional research, we were surprised to locate the original data for this braided flag which appeared from an area north of Grand Island. According, to the data, the flag had been left outside during a storm the day or two prior to the post. According to the review of Weather Underground at the Central Nebraska Regional Airport in Grand Island (KGRI), there were mild rain storms on and off the week prior to the braided flag event; however, the most significant storm occurred the day before from 1:00 am to 5:00 am. During this thunderstorm, the wind speed ranged from 16 mph to 32 mph with gusts ranging from 25 mph to 41 mph. The picture is very compelling.

Grand Island, Nebraska
Braided Flag

 Grand Island, Nebraska

The Bigfoot Field Research Organization (BFRO) maintains a Bigfoot Sightings Database on their website. According to their website, Nebraska has had a total of 15 Bigfoot sightings reported. Of particular note was a potential Bigfoot sighting on December 15, 1979 in St. Libory, NE about 20 miles North of Grand Island, NE. The witness stated that he was about 18 years old and living on a farm when the incident occurred. On approximately Dec. 15th, 1979 he was driving in his pickup to his mailbox which was at the end of a long driveway, when he saw a large man-like being with long, dark brown hair which was blowing in the strong northerly 30 mph wind. The witness stated that the being had long arms, had a large stride and was moving across the snow-covered field towards a shelterbelt with several trees. The location of this sighting is interesting considering it is also north of Grand Island and is about 70 miles directly west of Garrison, NE. The Platte River travels near Grand Island and is located north of Garrison, NE. In addition, there are many small rivers and creeks running throughout the area between Grand Island and Garrison.

Garrison, Nebraska
Braided Flag

Braided Windsocks, Marcola, Oregon

First letter and braided windsock received on 24-Dec-2020

To: Harriett McFeely,
1205 E. 42nd St., Hastings, NE
Phone: 402-463-6640

Hello Harriett,

A few weeks ago I saw an article on the internet about your Bigfoot Museum and enjoyed your stepping forth boldly with your collection and belief in "Biggie". I also believe but have never had proof; but, my daughter has seen one. My sons used to go hunting in the hills by our home and had certain areas where they avoided because they had creepy feelings that they were being watched. Once when they were older they ventured out into that area and found a large tall tree stump that was holowed out on one side with weeds and dry plants like padding that seemed to be quite a comfortable large chair or upright bed - - well they never needed to be told they were trespassing on someone's turf and have never gone near there again.

I live in the town of Marcola in the Mohawk Valley near Eugene, Oregon. You may have seen or heard in the news of the about the "Holiday Fire" that burned hundreds of acres near me in September.

https://www.facebook.com/HolidayFarmFire/

I worried about all the wild creatures and plants that were burned, harmed or killed along with all the homes and businesses that were destroyed. The fire was so close to our home that my son and I had to evacuate for a week until the fires were under control.

My son does advertising and promotions in parades etc. He has a big red pickup truck decorated with signs, banners and flags. (I have enclosed one of the decorations in this package for you) We never saw knots or braids in the tassles until after the Holiday Fire. The truck is parked close to our house. When my son went out to clean things up around here and saw the "tangled" strips on the flag he cut it off and brought in to me laughing about how "the wind tied knots in it when he was driving around". The wind never did that before and I was really excited to see the knots and braids because they were just like the ones you have at your museum. I went out and found a couple small knots on the other flags; so then I went out and checked every day to see if there were any more. Even though the truck was parked and not being moved for a couple of weeks I found a few more knots and then a couple of big ones appeared at the top of the display attached about eight foot up the poles. I rescued that artwork and decided to share one with you for your Bigfoot Museum.

I hope you enjoy it,
Yvonne

 Braided Windsocks, Marcola, Oregon

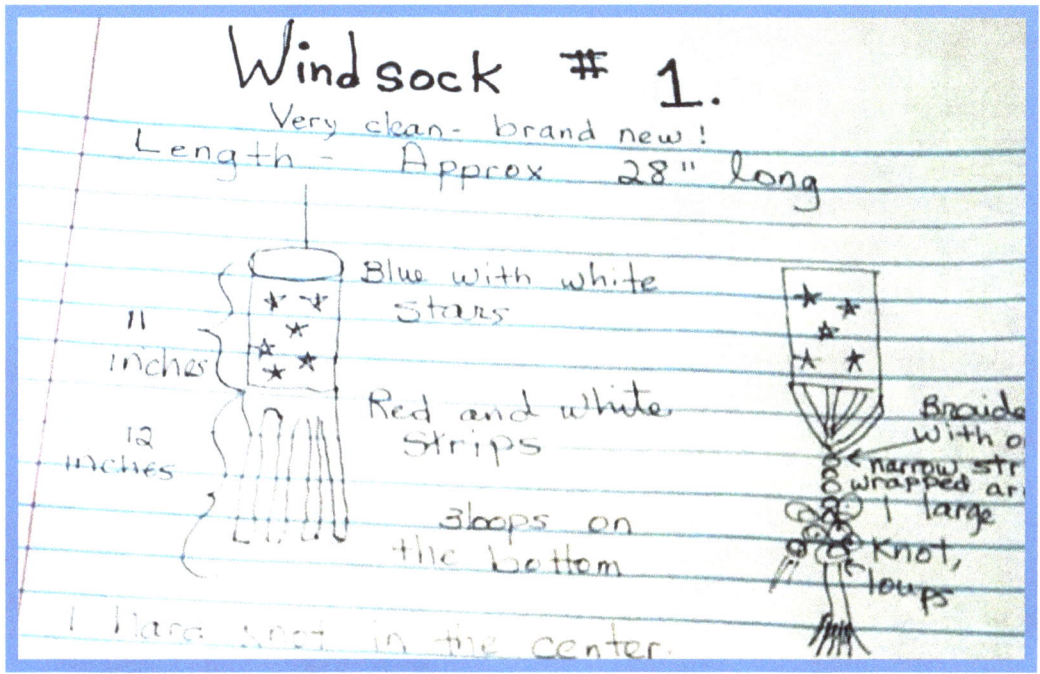

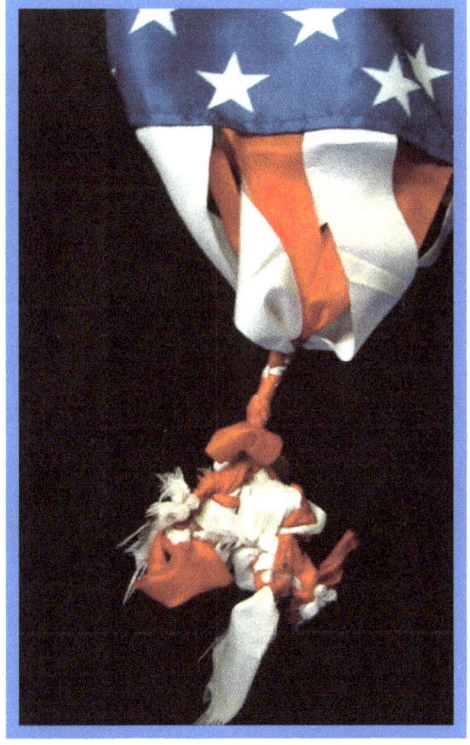

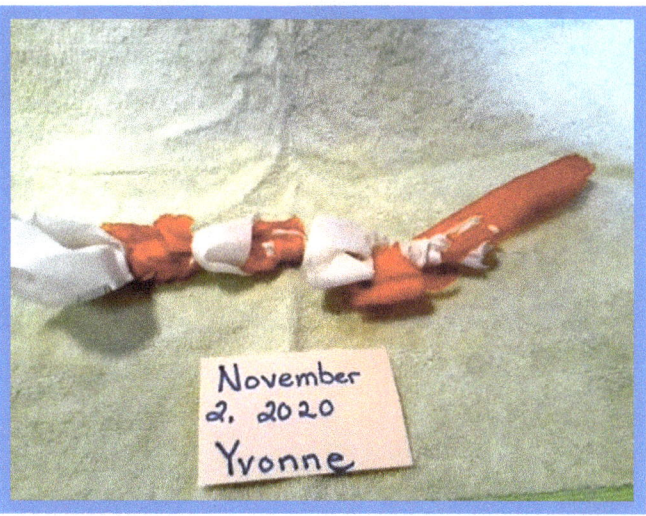

These windsocks were all in excellent condition.
They were clean and bright red, white and blue.

Braided Windsocks, Marcola, Oregon

December 27, 2020

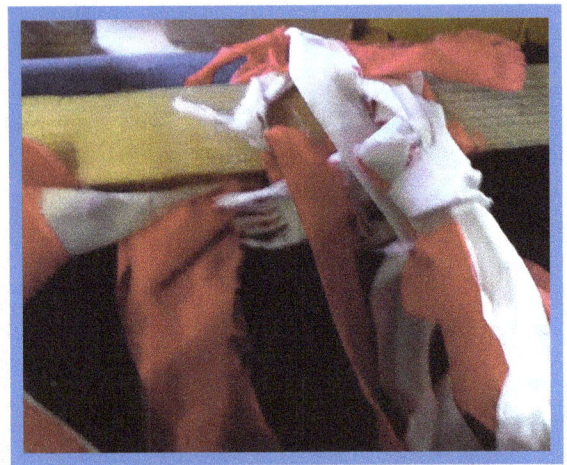

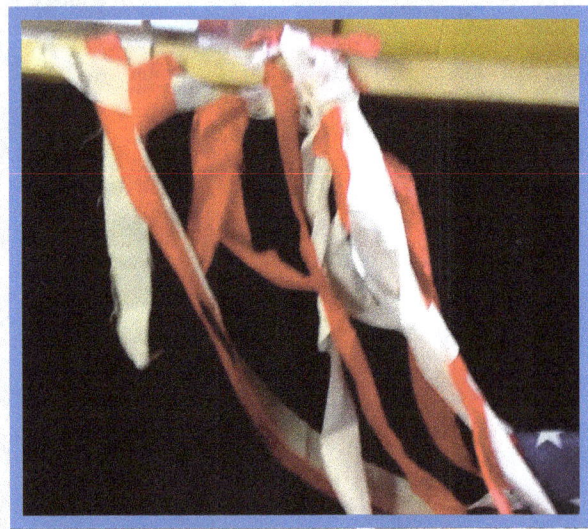

 Braided Windsocks, Marcola, Oregon

Comparison of the Oregon Braided Windsocks to the
13 Braided Flags from Butler County, Nebraska

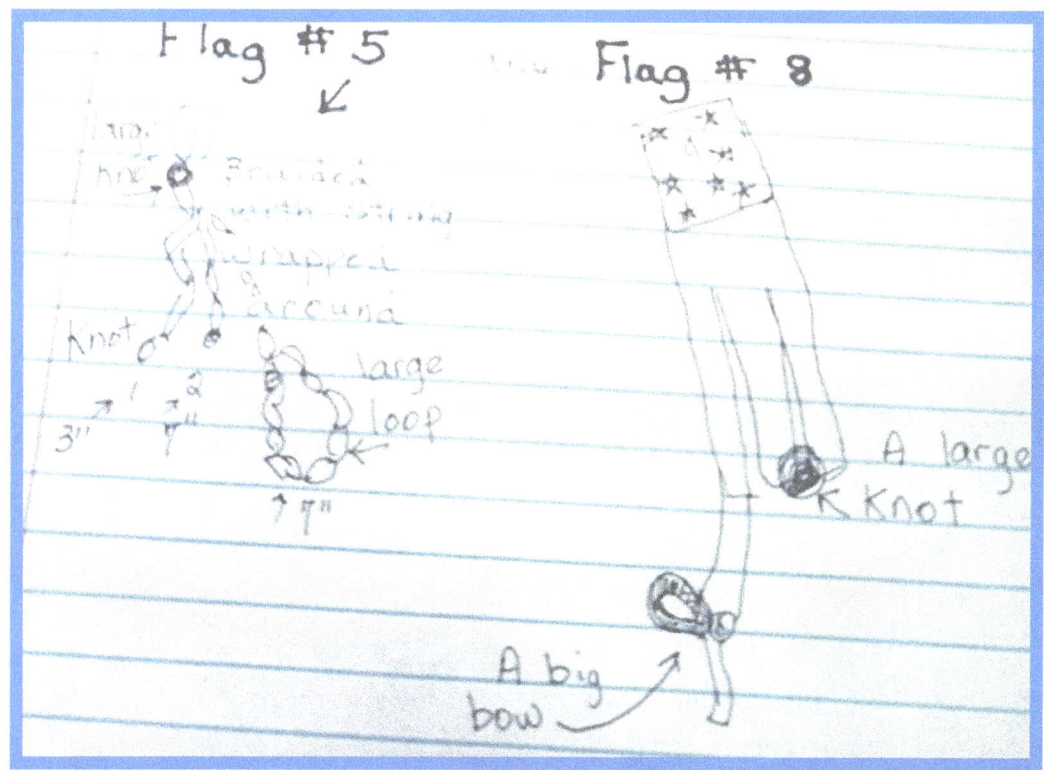

   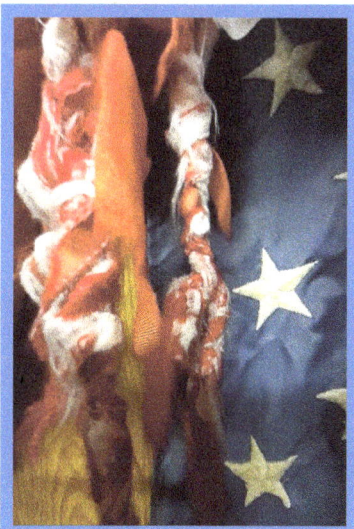   

Flag #5   *Flag #5*   *Flag #8*

 Braided Windsocks, Marcola, Oregon

Mrs. Yvonne Endersby

Yvonne's son's truck

Timeline

• September 7th 2020 – Start of the Holiday Fire in Lane County.

• The temperature averaged in the 80's degrees F daily until the smoke from the fire blocked out the sun – and then it cooled down to the 60's degrees F.

• The wind from the East was very strong for several days – then reversed to West and dropped to 1 to 2 mph.

• September 9th 2020 – the Endersby family was evacuated from their home for 6 days from September 9th to September 16th.

• The first knots were found on November 1st 2020, after that Yvonne checked for knots every day and some VERY LARGE ones appeared. These knots were braided overnight.

Mrs. Yvonne Endersby has agreed to keep us posted and her son will take pictures of all new events.

Things to notice:

1. Temperature was 60-65 degrees, nice fall weather.

2. The truck was parked next to the house and was well protected from winds.

3. Earlier in September 2020, extensive and very dangerous forest fires burned in the vicinity.

 Braided Windsocks, Marcola, Oregon

Yvonne had more instances of windsock braiding and provided photographs of these braided windsocks. In addition, she placed peanut butter as a gift; however, the peanut butter was not touched. A possible track was also photographed; however, the track is difficult to distinguish. A photograph of the location of the windsocks and possible track was provided for reference. The windsocks were located on the yellow sign on the trailer; however, this trailer had been parked and not driven anywhere before these windsocks were braided.

Braided Windsocks

During a search for additional braided flags on 03-Nov-2020 and 31-Jan-2021 several instances of braided windsocks were located. A total of 7 braided windsocks were reported across the United States during this search for flags as listed below.

- Shell Knob, Missouri – April 26, 2017
- Okeechobee, Florida – September 15, 2017
- Panama City, Florida - February 10, 2019
- Inyokern, California – November 14, 2017 and March 28, 2020
- Northville, Michigan – 22-Apr-2013 – four times in one week prior to this date
- Keels, Newfoundland and Labrador, Canada – August 19, 2017
- Chinook, Washington – 23-Dec-2020

Due to this research, Tamara Stier, Research Analyst, purchased a windsock and placed it outside with a trail camera on 08-Nov-2020. The location is outside of Omaha, Nebraska, to the northwest of Omaha. As of 25-Jan-2021, this windsock is not twisted, knotted, torn or braided. Strong winds are fairly common in Nebraska most of the year. According to NOAA in November 2020, the average wind speed was 10.6 mph with a maximum sustained wind speed of 32 mph and the maximum wind gust was 48 mph. In December 2020, the average wind speed was 9.05 mph with a maximum sustained wind speed of 39 mph and the maximum wind gust was 52 mph. In January 2021, the average wind speed was 9.3 mph and the maximum sustained wind speed was 36 mph and the maximum wind gust was 53 mph.

Brand new windsock in northwest part of Omaha

After temperature fluctuation, winds up to 53 mph, and snow, the windsock is STILL IN PERFECT CONDITION

 Opposable Thumbs?

"The wind did not do that."

My longtime friend Paco Elizalde stopped by the Museum and took a look at the flag from Garrison.

Someone had told him about the flag and said he thought the wind did it. After carefully examining the flag, Paco declared "The wind did not do that." He said that he was a certified storm chaser and was trained to identify different storms and cloud formations and the powerful strength that different storms can produce.

"Neither a wind, nor a vortex, nor a tornado has the ability to do braiding as intricate as was done on this flag, nor for that matter, to braid anything. Even in a tornado or strong winds, flags might be completely torn or shredded and even ripped down, but they were never braided. For anything to be braided, as the flags were, an entity has to do it, and that entity has to have both sufficient dexterity and the ability to grasp the strands."

Paco Elizalde is a retired Army Master Sergeant, a Vietnam Veteran and Purple Heart recipient, when he retired from the Army after 21 years of service Paco operated his own detective agency, which required him to be attentive to detail. He also volunteers for the Military Order of the Purple Heart, U.S.A., in which he assists Purple Heart recipients and other Veterans get their needs met. Paco has also been a professional game guide, for which he acquired the skills of tracking many species of animals in the wild.

For over eight years he has been an active Sasquatch researcher. He lives in the Denver area and is a member of Sasquatch Investigation of the Rockies (S.I.R.) team. Paco has had a few encounters with Sasquatches in Wyoming and Colorado mountain ranges, and has never felt intimidated or in danger by them.

 # Braided Ropes

Braided ropes are being found in farmers' barns, Quonsets, on machinery, saddles, and bridles, martingales, and around deer antlers. One man found a rope tied on every step of a ladder!!

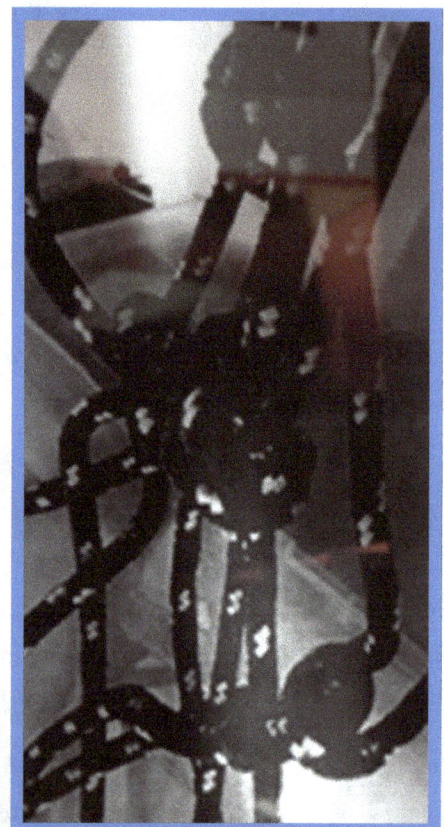

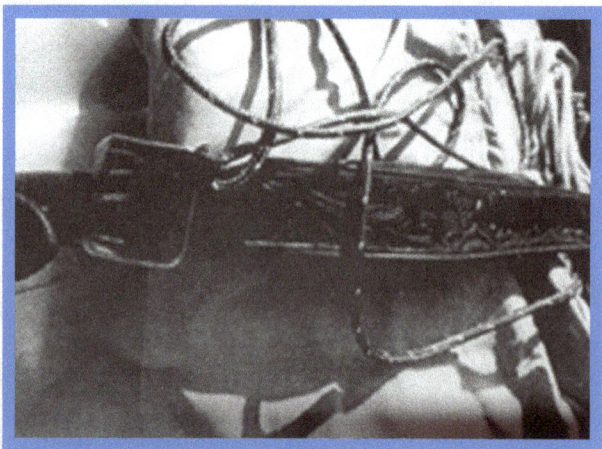

Braided Ropes

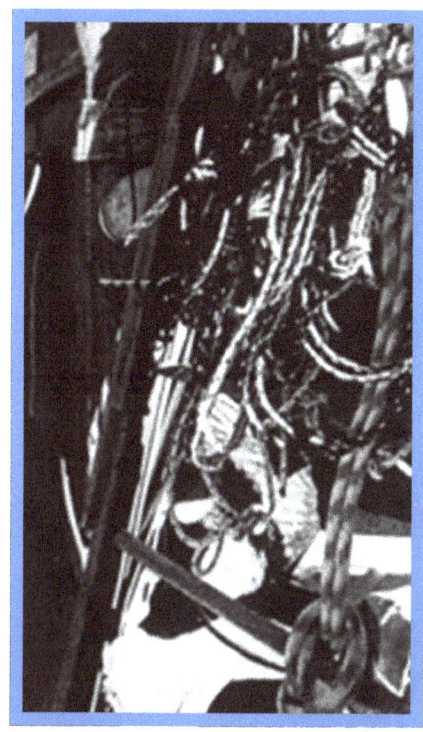

 A Historic Flag Mystery

One day a gentleman arrived at the museum for a tour and provided me a pamphlet from dedication of the Superior-Courtland Diversion Dam at Guide Rock on the Republican River. This pamphlet has a surprise, with a mention of 97 giant skeletons discovered in 1925 at a Guide Rock Native American burial mound. The article states that the first inhabitants of the area were known as "Tahoes," which were a tribe of giant people with many tribe members' height between 8 and half to 9 feet tall. This pamphlet suggests that Mr. A. T. Hill discovered these remains, and on looking deeper we learned that Mr. Hill was led to this location in his quest to solve a mystery about the first U.S. Flag flown over the land that is now Nebraska. His studies led him to become one of the 'giants' of Nebraska archaeology.

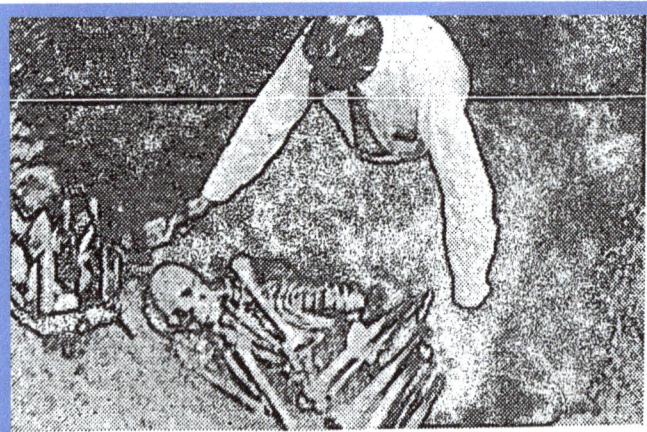

Indian grave opened by A. T. Hill (man in picture) about 1925. One of many found in Guide Rock burial ground. Many such skeletons were victims of a scourge of small pox, contracted by association with white men, which decimated the red men in great numbers.

Early People In The Republican Valley
By Thos. H. Vaughan

Mr. Asa Thomas Hill examining a skeleton in southern Nebraska, ca 1925. The circumstances of this photograph prior to the pamphlet are not yet known to us.

A. T. Hill (1871-1953) was a pioneer of systematic archaeology in the Great Plains, especially Nebraska, and from 1933 until 1949 served as Director of the Museum and Field Archeology for the Nebraska State Historical Society.[1] Though schooled only through the fourth grade, he made himself into a very well educated man and his efforts introduced a scientific approach into Nebraska archaeology of the day; he greatly influencing his own and succeeding generations of historians and archaeologists.

---

[1] https://www.nebraskahistory.org/lib-arch/research/manuscripts/family/asa-hill.htm. Retrieved March 4, 2021

A Historic Flag Mystery

A. T. Hill's curiosity was aroused when he attended the 1906 dedication ceremony for a site in Kansas identified as the Pawnee village where Zebulon Pike persuaded the chiefs to first raise the American flag in the territory.[1] Upon reading Pike's diary of the encounter, Hill was convinced that the location was incorrect, and in his travels Hill eventually found a place that fit much better. This site near Guide Rock, Nebraska, is now called the 'Pike-Pawnee Village' or 'Hill Farm' site. The latter name was given because A. T. Hill purchased the land there in order to preserve it, and there he began carefully collecting and cataloging artifacts of the ancient inhabitants, which in turn led to his role with the Nebraska State Historical Society.

ERECTED BY THE STATE OF KANSAS
1901
To mark the site of the Pawnee Republic, where
LIEUT. ZEBULON M. PIKE
caused the Spanish flag to be lowered
and the flag of the United States to be raised,
September 29, 1806

The marker in Republic County, Kansas commemorating the Pawnee village in which the American flag was raised. Though this was a notable event, it evidently occurred in a different location.

The site A. T. Hill had discovered was gradually accepted as the correct one, and its location has been designated a National Historic Site, as described by this plaque in the town of Guide Rock.[2]

There is evidence of numerous habitations on this site and many burials also. But did A. T. Hill find the bones of ancient giants? **If not, then where did Mr. Vaughn get the idea to write it into his pamphlet?** A colleague commented that Hill had an "aversion to setting down in print what he had seen or inferred."[3] So, we don't know what he chose not to print.

Hill solved one 'flag question' but we are left with more 'weird' questions…

---

1   Photo by Ammodramus, Public domain, via Wikimedia Commons. https://commons.wikimedia.org/wiki/File:Pawnee_Indian_Museum_(Republic,_Kansas)_monument_2.JPG
2   By Ammodramus - Own work, Public Domain, https://commons.wikimedia.org/wiki/File:Guide_Rock,_Nebraska_Pike_marker.JPG
3   Wedel, Waldo (1953). "Pioneer Nebraska Archeologist". Nebraska History, vol. 34, pp. 71-79

A Historic Flag Mystery

Site of the first raising of the U.S. Flag in Nebraska?

" "... it was impossible for the [Pawnee] nation to have two fathers; that they must either be the children of the Spaniards, or acknowledge their American father." After a silence of some time an old man rose, went to the door, took down the Spanish flag, brought it and laid it at my feet; he then received the American flag, and elevated it on the staff which had lately borne the standard of his Catholic Majesty"

Lt. Zebulon Pike[1]

Guide Rock. Located south of the Republican River, and a few miles east of the former Pawnee village

Plaque at the village site near Guide Rock identified by A. T. Hill.

Near the site, by unknown artist.

"It is my belief that this site marks the Pike-Pawnee Council which resulted in the hauling down of the Spanish flag and raising of the Stars and Stripes on the Nebraska-Kansas plains,..."

A. T. Hill, Nebraska History Magazine, 1927 p167.

---

1   Quoted in Platoff, Anne M., The Pike-Pawnee Flag Incident: Reexamining a Vexillological Legend, Raven: A Journal of Vexillology, 6 (1999).

Nebraska Giants

Dedication OF SUPERIOR-COURTLAND DIVERSION DAM AT GUIDE ROCK

GUIDE ROCK, NEBR., AUG. 17th 1950

The pamphlet contributed by a Museum visitor.[1]

He told us it had been received by his father, who attended the dedication ceremony, and tucked away in a trunk with other memorabilia and stored in the attic for decades. The gentleman inherited this trunk full of small items and years later went through it to sort things out. Finding this pamphlet he thought it would be of interest to us at the museum. It sure is!

---

1 Thomas Vaughan, US Bureau of Reclamation. Believed to have been distributed at dedication ceremony, 1950.

Nebraska Giants

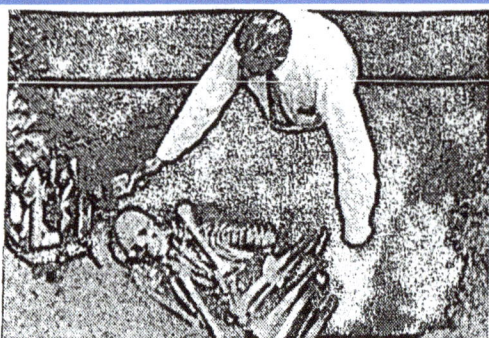

Indian grave opened by A. T. Hill (man in picture) about 1925. One of many found in Guide Rock burial ground. Many such skeletons were victims of a scourge of small pox, contracted by association with white men, which decimated the red men in great numbers.

Early People In The Republican Valley

By Thos. H. Vaughan

It is a matter of conjecture as to just what Chief Caracterish might be thinking, should he come to life today and stand on a bluff of the Republican River and cast his eyes up and down the valley. What might be his impressions when he sees a giant machine cutting large bites out of a hill, and in a few hours the land is level? Or other machines digging in the mud of the river and making a place for the white man's dam, in his great scheme to harness the river?

Chief Caracterish was head of the Pawnee Nation in 1806, when Lieut. Zebulon Pike visited his headquarters on the Republican about six miles west of "guide rock", which was then a huge rocky hill on the south bank of the river.

The first known red men here were the Tahoes, a giant tribe of people of great stature, many of the men being 8½ to 9 feet tall. They were here before the Pawnees, who came approximately 225 years ago. These giant men were said to go on the prairie when they wanted meat, capture a buffalo bare-handed by grabbing the creature by the horns, twisting its head and breaking its neck.

For some reason, possibly because of their warlike tendencies, even fighting among each other, these giants disappeared. They apparently also were decimated for lack of intelligence in battling the forces of nature.

Several years ago, A. T. Hill of the State Historical Society, uncovered a huge grave on top of the "guide rock" in which he found 97 bodies of the giant red men. Doubtless, there are other great common graves of these people situated in as yet undiscovered places on the string of hills along the Republican.

The Pawnees came north from the borders of Mexico. They were many years in coming. Between what are now the Republican and Solomon valleys lay a wonderful country. It was the red man's paradise. Survivors of the tribe, living in Oklahoma in recent years, tell stories to their children of this wonderland, stories handed down by word-of-mouth from generation to generation. Here in these fertile valleys the Indian women grew corn, pumpkin, squash, melons and beans. A favorite dish was buffalo meat cooked with corn and pumpkin, which they ate without seasoning. Their main food was buffalo and deer from the prairie, and fish and turtle from the river.

The Pawnees were the most cultured of all Indian tribes. Pawnees never attacked white settlers. White men felt safe when they had settled close to a Pawnee village, for these people protected them from their common enemies, the warlike Sioux and Cheyennes. The Pawnees were advanced in medicine and music, many of them making crude musical instruments used extensively in serenading at their evening campfire gatherings. Their medicine men learned the value of certain herbs, grasses and the bark of certain trees.

The Pawnee nation was divided into four tribes, each of which had an Indian and a white man's name: Chau-i, Grand; Kitke-hah-i, Republican; Pita-hau-crat, Noisy; and Ski-di, Wolf. These tribes were divided into bands and lived in groups of houses, keeping together when on the march.

The Pawnees were a religious people. Their god was Tirawa, Great One in the Sky, whom they supplicated in times of battle or during a drouth. In those early years a stream of water was said to flow under the "guide rock", which became one of their places of worship for

---

Thomas Vaughan mentions Hill's finding of skeletal remains of ancient apparently 'giant' people in the Republican River valley. The denotation 'Tahoe' is not currently in use for either a modern or Paleo-Indian tribe, so we don't know who they were or where the author got that information.

 Nebraska Giants

the reason that their brothers, the birds of the air, the animals of the field, and the denizens of the deep, could meet here in council. It was said that many decisions were made by a giant turtle which inhabited the river. If the turtle took to the land, the warriors decided to attack; on the other hand, if the turtle chose to dig down in the mud of the river, the decision was otherwise.

Around the year 1800, the Pawnees were the most numerous and powerful nation of the plains. They were decimated largely because of their peace loving ways. They were constantly being attacked by the Sioux and Cheyennes, who coveted their horses and beautiful women. Other enemies were the Utes, Commanches, Arapahoes and Blackfeet, the latter being from the far Northwest, who came at times to hunt buffalo on the Plains.

In 1880 the Pawnees numbered around 10,000 people. Lieutenant Pike writes in his memoirs that there were around 2,000 of them in the head village at "guide rock" when he visited Chief Caracterish in September, 1806.

The object of Pike's travels was to visit the head chief of the Pawnee Nation and persuade him to take down the Spanish flag, and in its place hoist the Stars and Stripes. Pike was sent on this mission by President Thomas Jefferson. Pike did not meet physical resistance but there was unrest among the warriors. He marched his twenty men across the river and dug pits from which they might defend themselves in case of attack. The older men of the tribe were finally convinced that Pike's message was true. Later, in October, Pike and his men marched boldly toward the setting sun, where he discovered the mountain peak which now bears his name. In 1833 the Pawnees ceded to the United States Government all lands south of the Platte River.

In 1857, cholera attacked the tribe, and 1,200 men, women and children succumbed. The tribes were now living on the Loup rivers, north of the Platte, and in 1859 the entire nation numbered less than 4,000. The following fourteen years were full of misfortune and disaster. They were frequently attacked by their old enemies, the Sioux, when their women dared not hoe in the fields. In 1873, 86 Pawnees were killed by the Sioux, while on a buffalo hunt near Culbertson. In 1874, the remaining 1500 Pawnees drifted southward toward the Indian Territory to live near the friendly tribe of Wichitas, arriving there the following year.

For a number of years the Pawnees died rapidly. Living in a land that was more cloudy and damp they have succumbed, until today there is but a remnant left. Heart-broken and homesick for the land of flowing rivers and beautiful hills, they became rapidly less in number.

To the children of this noble people, Nebraska is a wonderful land, full of magical places, the scene of heroic battles and strange events in their history.

This is the story of the people who once walked where we now walk. They are the people who once lived on this prairie in sod houses made much like the sod houses the white man built later, except that they were circular in shape, and had an opening in the roof instead of a chimney; an opening used for a door in the southeast facing the rising sun; earthern shelves or beds built around the sides; a pit in the northwest, opposite the door, in which food was stored; a campfire in the center around which they gathered at evening to visit.

Most of the Republican valley was settled by white men in the 1870's. We have now lived here 80 years. The Indian owned the land in common; the white man fences off a parcel and claims it as his own personally. The white man posts "no trespassing" signs which are ignored by corn borers, chinch bugs and grass hoppers. The white man owns a house or parcel of land on which he pays taxes and then gnashes his teeth. The Indian hunted his food and fished in the river as he pleased; the white man buys a duck stamp, a ten-dollar reel and a seventy-five dollar gun, then comes home and buys his meat at the market.

"Ugh! White man think him heap smart!"

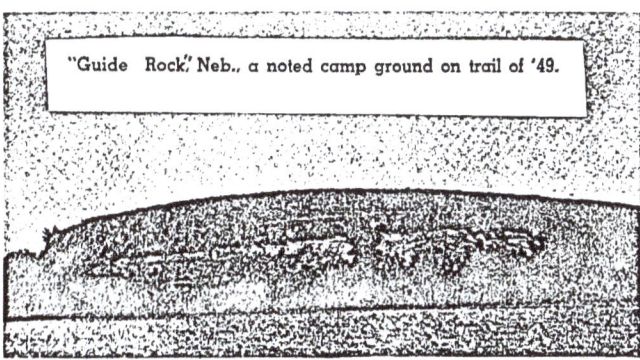

"Guide Rock," Neb., a noted camp ground on trail of '49.

Ron Morehead

Hi Harriett,

For many years I didn't reveal this picture because it is so difficult to believe. But it is what it is, e.g., real, huge. We witnessed it while hunting. It was made about ½ mile from our camp and we were not prepared to cast it. We didn't see the being that made it, but it was fresh and we had to assume it was at least 12 feet tall…probably more like 15 feet. There is a theory that suggests their pituitary gland is not limited as a human's….we get so big and we stop growing. This attribute would also account for the historical explanations of these creatures getting very, very tall.

It was definitely not human…not like ours. I believe them to be hybrid with their mtDNA at 100%. Their nuDNA is currently unknown and would be dependent on what aliens manipulated their genome of the attributes. Lucky us, we were created in the image of a very special entity and been given dominion on this planet…not them.

My Best,

Ron Morehead

Thoughts

    I have been thinking, about this... first we have the flag, then we have the horses, then the windsocks. Then the last thing is the ropes...I think all of these things illustrate that the BIGFOOT are very artistic. In addition, there are "Arches, A's, X's and glyphs." They also seem to like the colors red and blue...but more red... I don't know if this is a preference or just a coincidence...

    I also wonder if we need to change our attitude.. we consider these torn, braided and knotted flags an act of vandalism.. BUT, DO THE BIGFOOT, OR WHOEVER OR WHATEVER who is doing this... do they consider it vandalism???? Or, do they consider it a part of 'staking out their territory'? Or, is it a piece of artwork like the huge A's and X's they make??? Here in America, we 'brand' our cattle. In ancient China, each family group had their own distinctive braid so they could identify their animals... and here in AMERICA, many of the Native American tribes are very artistic, and they make beautiful, intricate baskets and other items made out of horsehair, sweet grass and straw. So could the flags be a variation of artwork??? When ropes are found in barns and other buildings, they are very detailed, and often they incorporate things they find in the barn; bridles, martingale, antlers, pitch forks, and curry combs.... None of these items are destroyed... they are just a piece of the artwork.. And when Igor suggested putting colored ribbons out in the corral, it wasn't long before they "showed up" braided into the horses manes.!!! That was NOT VANDALISM; That was a piece of art!!

Thoughts

Everything we see depends upon our own individual perspective. For example, my friend Dan Nedrelo was here at the MUSEUM a few years ago. He had with him a white, albino snake named Ice that was over 5 feet long.!!! He had been looking for a woman to hold her and then he could take some pictures. (Dan is a professional photographer and Herpetologist.) I said, "I can hold her!" Which I did! She was very nice and gentle and not 'slimy.' And Dan got some good pictures. Dan loves that snake.. other people would never even touch her or hold her. (That is individual perspective.)

Harriett and Ice

They would faint, or scream, or run away, or try to kill her...... you see, it all depends on your perspective...... And, last, I wonder, COULD THIS BE A FORM OF GIFTING??? ALL OF THESE FLAGS have been out in plain sight, not hidden. NOTHING ELSE has been damaged or destroyed.. I am reminded of the many times when we have been out camping and sleeping in a tent... "They" have walked around our tent (we heard them) and they left footprints.. they opened the cooler several times and looked at the ketchup and mustard and other things, BUT they never broke anything or took anything... they just closed the lid...AND ONCE, they left a beautiful bowl. Only ½ of it was there, and on the bottom it said 1937!!! Where did they find that in the middle of the mountains??? They have given pine cones, bouquets of flowers, sweet grass, obsidian rocks, sea shells, 1880 blue glass bottles and cotton balls!! So, I wonder, are the flags a gift? A sign of friendship or acceptance? Are these new territories for them??????

I wonder............H.

 Thoughts

I surely think that Ron must hold the world's record for size and stride! And I am constantly amazed this creature was near their camp, so he had to have known that Ron and the others were there... But, he NEVER disturbed anything, and he NEVER hurt anyone...

Don Monroe believes there are many wild, feral beings 'out there' among us... He has seen many 'weird' things for which there is no explanation...and so have many others!

In the end, perhaps we should go back to the beginning:

Genesis 6:4 says:

In those days, AND EVEN AFTERWARDS, when the evil beings from the spirit world were sexually involved with human women, their children became GIANTS, of whom so many legends are told.

Could the key words be EVEN AFTERWARDS?

The giants are often referred to as the Nephilim. I have thought for many years that all of this information is just pieces of a giant puzzle. The videos, photographs, pictures, footprints, bones, howls, screams, tree breaks, arches, burial mounds, books, gifts, RESEARCHERS and EXPLORERS are all part of a GIANT PUZZLE. WE are al just a small piece, but we are all very important. I think gradually these pieces are coming together and then perhaps we will know as Paul Harvey used to say, THE REST OF THE STORY.

Please evaluate the TRUE stories, the witnesses and the pictures.

I am giving you the current evidence which could change in a heartbeat TODAY or TOMORROW...

Draw your own conclusions and make up your mind...

    Much Love,

    Harriett,

    The Bigfoot Lady

Conclusions

......Nevertheless, what is here, down for the record may prove to be the only true important and a very first stepping stone into all future plaiting discoveries that will completely jam wide open the long, locked doors of Pandora's mysterious box???

Don Monroe

We all have our opinions and what we believe is substantial evidence to support them. So, NOW I will submit this for your approval and analysis; inviting you to draw your own individual conclusions as to what may have occurred that 'WEIRD,' fateful, MEMORIAL DAY WEEKEND in the CEMETERY...GARRISON, NEBRASKA.

Harriett McFeely
The Bigfoot Lady

AND,
As Don Monroe says...........*"ALWAYS EXPECT THE UNEXPECTED!"*

 # AND

AND

Should you decide to go for a late night stroll down by the cemetery…

AND

If you witness any blood curdling, terrifying screams, OR anything that seems 'WEIRD,' please let me know. I and my TEAM would LOVE to explore and investigate further!!

You can call me at the

Bigfoot Crossroads of America Museum and Research Center at

402-705-0000

In Hastings, Nebraska

Harriett McFeely
The Bigfoot Lady